Emma Lane

THE EASIEST DIABETIC DIET AFTER 60

A Science-Backed Cookbook for Managing Blood Sugar and Heart Health | Delicious Recipes and Meal Plan for Prediabetes, Type 2 Diabetes, and the Newly Diagnosed

CONTENTS

THEORY

BREAKFAST 29

LUNCH 35

DINNER 41

SNACK   47

DESSERT   53

THEORY

CONCLUSION

INTRODUCTION

Welcome to *The Easiest Diabetic Diet After 60*, a guide designed with you in mind. Whether you've recently been diagnosed with prediabetes or type 2 diabetes, or you're seeking to manage your health more effectively, this book is here to empower you.

As someone who values wellness and practical advice, **my approach is rooted in science** and tailored specifically for adults over 60. From my own experience, I know that **managing blood sugar levels** and **maintaining heart health** can sometimes feel overwhelming, especially with the myriad of conflicting dietary information available online.

This book aims to cut through that confusion, offering clear, actionable guidance that fits seamlessly into your life. I understand that your goal is to live independently, stay active in your community, and enjoy every day to its fullest. That's why I've filled these pages with easy-to-implement strategies, delectable recipes, and a comprehensive meal plan that caters to your needs.

WHAT MAKES THIS BOOK DIFFERENT?

For starters, it's about **practicality**. Drastic lifestyle changes or obscure ingredients won't cut it. You need solutions that are simple, effective, and enjoyable. The recipes included in this book are healthy and delicious, plus they are easy to prepare. Your time is valuable, and maintaining consistency in your dietary habits shouldn't mean spending hours in the kitchen or hunting down exotic foods.

As you navigate *The Easiest Diabetic Diet After 60*, you'll discover a wealth of tips designed to help you stay on track. From strategies for dining out without compromising your health to finding inspiration from success stories, every section aims to support your journey toward better health.

You'll learn how to involve your family in healthier eating habits, making mealtime a shared, supportive experience. You'll see that the path to well-being is much easier when traveling with loved ones by your side.

RECIPE LAYOUT: FOCUSING ON YOUR HEALTH

Let's talk about structure. Each recipe comes **with detailed information on servings, serving size, and nutritional content.** This ensures that you have a clear understanding of what you're eating and how it impacts your health. The meal plans focus on balance and moderation and they are crafted to help you manage your blood sugar levels while enjoying flavorful, satisfying meals.

APPROACHABLE AND SUSTAINABLE DIETARY CHANGES

The goal of *The Easiest Diabetic Diet After 60* is to provide you with everything you need to take control of your health—making dietary changes approachable and sustainable. It's not just about following a diet; it's about adopting a lifestyle that promotes long-term well-being. With science-backed advice, you can trust that the guidance offered here is reliable and effective.

Throughout this book, you'll find encouragement to connect with your community. Engaging with others who share similar health challenges can be incredibly motivating. Whether it's participating in local wellness programs or simply sharing a meal with friends who understand your journey, these connections can enhance your commitment to a **healthier lifestyle**.

Your health is a priority, and managing diabetes doesn't have to feel like an uphill battle. This book offers you the tools to make it manageable and even enjoyable. The practical advice, tested recipes, and meal plans within these pages are here to simplify your life and enhance your **well-being**. You deserve to feel great and live fully, and this book is here to support you every step of the way.

WHAT YOU'LL FIND IN THIS BOOK

When you're busy exploring the chapters ahead, know that you're not alone. Many other adults have walked this path before you and found success through consistent, mindful choices. Their stories serve as inspiration and proof that with the right approach, managing diabetes is entirely achievable. When you decide to integrate these practices into your daily routine, you set yourself up for a future where health challenges do not define your life but become just another aspect that you manage with grace and confidence.

We'll journey through the following chapters:

1. Understanding Diabetes and Its Impact After 60

2. Essential Nutrients and Foods for Diabetic Seniors

3. Creating a Balanced Meal Plan

4. Delicious and Easy Recipes

5. Lifestyle Tips for Managing Diabetes

I'm going to empower you with the knowledge and **practical tools** you need on your journey. The recipes are designed to please your taste buds while **supporting your health goals**. I've avoided trends and fads, opting instead to bring you methods that are proven and trusted. This book is not about restriction; it's about celebrating the abundance of flavors and nutritious options available to you.

As you turn each page, you're taking an important step toward better health. I'm excited to accompany you on this journey, providing support, guidance, and delicious meals along the way. *The Easiest Diabetic Diet After 60* is more than just a cookbook; it's a companion in your quest for a healthier, more vibrant life.

BONUS RESOURCES TO SUPPORT YOUR DIABETES MANAGEMENT JOURNEY

Before we dive into the wealth of information this book offers, I'm excited to provide you with some valuable additional resources to enhance your diabetes management journey. I understand that managing diabetes is a continuous process, and extra support can make a huge difference. That's why I've prepared a set of free, downloadable resources to complement this book:

1. *Festive Feasts: Diabetes-Friendly Recipes for Special Occasions* — An ebook filled with low-GI recipes and menu plans for celebrations.

2. *Move More, Stress Less: Exercise Guide for Diabetes Management* — This ebook offers low-impact exercises tailored for seniors with diabetes.

3. *Breathe Easy: A Guide to Quitting Smoking for People with Diabetes* — Learn about the specific benefits of quitting smoking when you have diabetes, along with practical strategies to help you quit.

4. *Access to 20 easy-to-follow video recipes* tailored for diabetes management.

These resources are designed to provide more in-depth guidance on specific aspects of diabetes management, helping you put the knowledge from this book into practice.

TO ACCESS THESE FREE RESOURCES, SIMPLY SCAN THE QR CODE:

We recommend bookmarking this page for easy reference. As you progress through the book, you'll find these additional materials particularly helpful in implementing the strategies and advice provided.

Thank you for trusting me with your health. Let's start on this journey, one tasty meal at a time. With every bite, every choice, you'll be moving closer to a balanced, fulfilling lifestyle. Now, let's begin our journey to better diabetes management together!

1. UNDERSTANDING DIABETES AND ITS IMPACT AFTER 60

Let's start with the basics. If you're reading this, you likely have diabetes or are at risk of developing it. As you age, you need to understand what's happening in your body. This chapter cuts through the medical jargon to give you a clear picture of diabetes and how it affects you differently now that you're over 60. We'll discuss the types of diabetes, why diet matters so much, and the specific hurdles you face as a senior.

No sugar-coating here – just straightforward facts and practical insights. By the end of this chapter, you'll have the knowledge you need to take control of your health. This isn't about scaring you; it's about arming you with information. Let's dive in and lay the groundwork for the strategies we'll explore in the rest of the book.

WHAT IS DIABETES?

Diabetes is a condition where your body struggles to manage blood sugar levels. It's not just about having too much sugar in your blood—it's about how your body handles that sugar.

TYPES OF DIABETES

The following types of diabetes exist:

- **Type 1 diabetes:** Your body doesn't make insulin. It's less common and usually starts earlier in life, but it can happen at any age.

- **Type 2 diabetes:** Your body doesn't use insulin well. This is the most common type, especially in people over 60.

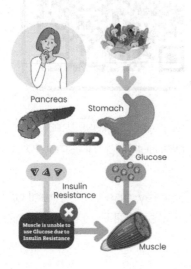

sugar levels are higher than normal but not high enough to be diagnosed as type 2 diabetes. It's a warning sign and a risk factor for developing type 2 diabetes (that's why I'm mentioning it here.)

- **Gestational diabetes:** This type occurs only during pregnancy, typically developing in the second or third trimester, and usually resolves after giving birth. While it's not directly relevant at our age, it's worth noting that women who've had gestational diabetes are at higher risk of developing type 2 diabetes later in life, making regular screening important for them.

- **Prediabetes:** Prediabetes is not a type of diabetes. It's a condition where blood

HOW DIABETES DEVELOPS

Type 2 diabetes, which you're most likely dealing with, develops gradually. Over the years, your cells become **resistant to insulin**, the hormone that helps sugar enter your cells. Your pancreas tries to make more insulin to compensate, but eventually, it can't keep up. The result? Too much sugar floating around in your bloodstream.

COMMON SYMPTOMS

Pay attention to certain symptoms that may indicate an underlying health issue. It's wise not to ignore the following signs:

Increased Thirst Coupled With Frequent Urination

When your body is trying to manage high blood sugar levels, it can lead to excessive thirst. People often find themselves drinking more fluids and visiting the bathroom more often than usual. If you notice that you are always **thirsty** and **urinating more frequently**, it may be time to consult with a healthcare provider.

Constant Fatigue

This feeling goes beyond just being tired after a long day's work. It is a persistent sense of weariness and **lack of energy** that does not seem to improve with rest. You may feel drained, making it difficult to carry out daily activities. If you find yourself unusually tired without a clear reason, explore this further with a medical professional.

Don't Overlook Blurred Vision

When blood sugar levels are high, they can affect the lenses of the eyes, causing them to swell. This swelling changes the way light is focused and can lead to unclear or fuzzy vision. If you experience episodes of **blurred vision**, especially if they happen frequently or last for extended periods, it is essential to get your eyes checked by a doctor.

Slow-Healing Wounds

If you notice that minor cuts or scrapes are taking longer than usual to heal, it might be worth investigating further. The healing process can be hindered for various reasons, including **poor blood circulation** or **infection**. Keeping an eye on how your body responds to injuries can provide valuable insight into your overall health.

Unexplained Weight Loss (Despite Eating More)

It is normal for people to lose weight when they are less active or if they are on a diet. However, if you are eating plenty of food and still losing weight, this could indicate a serious problem. **Weight loss** can occur when the body isn't able to **process food properly**, leading to a lack of essential nutrients. If this situation arises, seeking advice from a healthcare provider is crucial.

Numbness or Tingling in the Hands or Feet Should Not be Dismissed

This sensation can range from mild to severe and can affect one or both sides of the body. It is often a result of **nerve damage**, which can be caused by several factors, including high blood sugar levels. If you frequently experience numbness or tingling, seek guidance from a health professional, as this symptom may change how your body functions.

These symptoms can be subtle and easy to overlook. Many people might not recognize these signs or think they are part of a normal lifestyle. Understanding your symptoms is the first step to better health. Pay attention to your body; changes in how you feel can indicate a larger problem that may be addressed early.

Go for regular check-ups, as healthcare providers can perform tests and provide evaluations that identify potential health issues early on. Make it a habit to discuss any unusual changes with your doctor during check-ups to build a supportive relationship with your healthcare provider.

BLOOD SUGAR REGULATION AND INSULIN

Think of insulin as the key that unlocks your cells to let sugar in. When you eat, your blood sugar rises, and your pancreas releases insulin. This insulin helps move sugar from your blood into your cells, where it's used for energy.

In diabetes, with type 1, there's no key (insulin) at all. With type 2, the locks (cells) don't work well with the key (insulin resistance), or there aren't enough working keys (insulin deficiency). The result? Sugar builds up in your blood instead of entering your cells.Understanding diabetes is your first step in managing it effectively. It's not just about avoiding sugar—it's about how your body processes what you eat. In the next sections, we'll dive into why this matters even more after 60 and what you can do about it. Knowledge is power, and you're on your way to taking control of your health.

TYPES OF DIABETES AND THEIR DIFFERENCES

Let's explore the differences between the different types of diabetes by looking at their characteristics.

TYPE 1 DIABETES

This is the less common form, but it's important to understand. Here's what you need to know:

- Your body attacks and destroys insulin-producing cells in the pancreas
- It usually starts in childhood or young adulthood, but can occur at **any age**
- **Insulin injections are necessary** for survival
- It's not preventable and **not related to lifestyle factors**

TYPE 2 DIABETES

This is the most common type, especially for people over 60. Here's the deal:

- Your body becomes resistant to insulin or doesn't produce enough
- It **develops gradually**, often over years
- It's **influenced by** factors like **weight, diet, and physical activity**
- Many people can manage it with lifestyle changes and medication
- It's the type you're most likely to develop later in life

GESTATIONAL DIABETES

While less relevant to seniors, it's worth knowing about:

- Occurs during **pregnancy**
- Usually resolves after giving birth
- Increases the risk of developing type 2 diabetes later in life

PREVALENCE OF TYPE 2 DIABETES AMONG SENIORS

Face it—type 2 diabetes is common in your age group. Here's why:

- As you age, your body becomes less efficient at using insulin
- You may become less active, which affects how your body processes sugar
- Years of poor dietary habits can catch up with you
- About 1 in 4 adults over 65 has diabetes, and most of it is type 2 (Centers for Disease Control and Prevention, 2020)

Early detection is key. Many of us might already have prediabetes without knowing it. That's when your blood sugar is higher than normal but not high enough to be diagnosed as diabetes. It's a warning sign, but it also means you have a chance to turn things around.

Having diabetes doesn't mean your life is over. With proper management, which we'll get into later, you can still lead a full, active life. The first step is understanding what you're dealing with. Now that you know the types and why type 2 is so common among us seniors, we can move on to how to tackle it head-on.

THE IMPORTANCE OF DIET IN MANAGING DIABETES

Your diet plays an important role in managing diabetes. What you eat directly affects your blood sugar levels, making food choices an essential part of your diabetes care plan. Let's explore how diet impacts your health and what you can do to maintain stable blood sugar levels.

IMPACT OF DIET ON BLOOD SUGAR LEVELS

Different foods affect your blood sugar in different ways. Carbohydrates, particularly simple sugars, tend to raise blood sugar levels more quickly than proteins or fats. When you eat, your body breaks down carbohydrates into glucose, which enters your bloodstream. For those of you with diabetes, the body struggles to process this glucose effectively, leading to higher blood sugar levels.

THE IMPORTANCE OF A BALANCED DIET

A balanced diet is key to managing diabetes. It's not just about cutting out sugar; it's about creating a meal plan that provides your body with the right mix of nutrients. A well-balanced diet can help:

- **stabilize blood sugar levels**
- **maintain a healthy weight**
- **reduce the risk of diabetes-related complications**
- **improve overall health and energy levels**

GLYCEMIC INDEX CHART FOR DIABETICS

The glycemic index (GI) is a tool that can help you understand how different foods affect your blood sugar. Foods are ranked on a scale from 0 to 100, with higher numbers indicating a more rapid increase in blood sugar.

Here's a simplified GI chart:

- **Low GI (55 or less):** Most fruits and vegetables, beans, minimally processed grains
- **Medium GI (56-69):** Whole wheat products, brown rice, sweet corn
- **High GI (70 or above):** White bread, rice cakes, potatoes, pretzels

While the GI is helpful, it's not the only factor to consider. Portion sizes and overall meal composition also play important roles.

GLYCEMIC INDEX CHART

Grains and Starches

Low Glycemic Index (55 or less) Choose Most Often	Medium Glycemic Index (56 to 69) Choose Less Often	High Glycemic Index (70 or more) Choose Least Often
Breads: Heavy Mixed Grain Breads Spelt Bread Sourdough Bread Tortilla (Whole Grain) **Cereal:** All-Bran™ Cereal All-Bran Buds™ With Psyllium Cereal Oat Bran Oats (Steel Cut) **Grains:** Barley Bulgur Mung Bean Noodles Pasta (Al Dente, Firm) Pulse Flours Quinoa Rice (Converted, Parboiled) **Other:** Peas Popcorn Sweet Potato Winter Squash	**Breads:** Chapati (White, Whole Wheat) Flaxseed/Linseed Bread Pita Bread (White, Whole Wheat) Pumpernickel Bread Roti (White, Whole Wheat) Rye Bread (Light, Dark, Whole Grain) Stone Ground Whole Wheat Bread Whole Grain Wheat Bread **Cereal:** Cream of Wheat™ (Regular) Oats (Instant) Oats (Large Flake) Oats (Quick) **Grains:** Basmati Rice Brown Rice Cornmeal Couscous (Regular, Whole Wheat) Rice Noodles White Rice (Short, Long Grain) Wild Rice **Other:** Beets* Corn French Fries ⚠ Parsnip Potato (Red, White, Cooled) Rye Crisp Crackers (e.g. Ryvita Rye Crispbread™) Stoned Wheat Thins™ Crackers	**Breads:** Bread (White, Whole Wheat) Naan (White, Whole Wheat) **Cereal:** All-Bran Flakes™ Cereal Corn Flakes™ Cereal Cream of Wheat™ (Instant) Puffed Wheat Cereal Rice Krispies™ Cereal Special K™ Cereal **Grains:** Jasmine Rice Millet Sticky Rice White Rice (Instant) **Other:** Carrots* Potato (Instant Mashed) Potato (Red, White, Hot) Pretzels Rice Cakes Soda Crackers
Additional foods: 1. 2. 3.	**Additional foods:** 1. 2. 3.	**Additional foods:** 1. 2. 3.

Meat and Alternatives

Low Glycemic Index (55 or less) Choose Most Often	Medium Glycemic Index (56 to 69) Choose Less Often	High Glycemic Index (70 or more) Choose Least Often
Baked Beans	Lentil Soup (ready-made)	
Chickpeas	Split Pea Soup (ready-made)	
Kidney Beans		
Lentils		
Mung Beans		
Romano Beans		
Soybeans/Edamame		
Split Peas		
Additional foods:	**Additional foods:**	**Additional foods:**
1.	1.	1.
2.	2.	2.
3.	3.	3.

Milk, Alternatives and Other Beverages

Low Glycemic Index (55 or less) Choose Most Often	Medium Glycemic Index (56 to 69) Choose Less Often	High Glycemic Index (70 or more) Choose Least Often
Almond Milk		Rice Milk
Cow Milk		
(Skim, 1%, 2%, Whole)		
Frozen Yogurt ⚠		
Greek Yogurt		
Soy Milk		
Yogurt (Skim, 1%, 2%, Whole)		
Additional foods:	**Additional foods:**	**Additional foods:**
1.	1.	1.
2.	2.	2.
3.	3.	3.

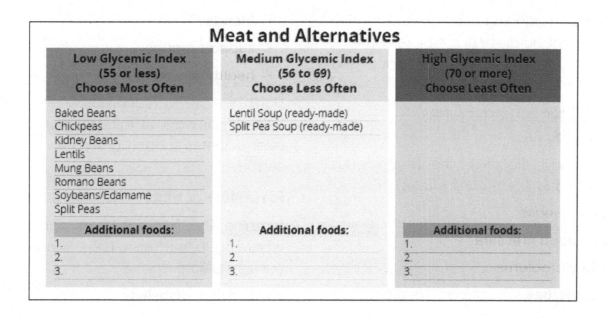

Meat and Alternatives

Low Glycemic Index (55 or less) Choose Most Often	Medium Glycemic Index (56 to 69) Choose Less Often	High Glycemic Index (70 or more) Choose Least Often
Baked Beans	Lentil Soup (ready-made)	
Chickpeas	Split Pea Soup (ready-made)	
Kidney Beans		
Lentils		
Mung Beans		
Romano Beans		
Soybeans/Edamame		
Split Peas		
Additional foods:	**Additional foods:**	**Additional foods:**
1.	1.	1.
2.	2.	2.
3.	3.	3.

FOODS TO LIMIT OR AVOID

While no foods are strictly off-limits, some should be consumed in moderation:

- sugary drinks and sodas
- processed snack foods
- white bread, rice, and pasta
- full-fat dairy products
- foods high in saturated and trans fats
- alcohol (can interfere with blood sugar control and medication)

Work with your healthcare provider or a registered dietitian to create a meal plan that works for you. They can help you balance your favorite foods with healthier alternatives and guide you on appropriate portion sizes.

Managing diabetes through diet doesn't mean eliminating all the foods you love. It's about making informed choices and finding a balance that keeps you healthy while still enjoying your meals. In the next sections, we'll discuss specific dietary strategies and meal-planning tips to help you take control of your diabetes.

CHALLENGES FACED BY SENIORS WITH DIABETES

As you age, managing diabetes comes with its own set of hurdles. Let's explore some of the unique challenges you are facing and how to address them.

COMMON COMORBIDITIES IN SENIORS WITH DIABETES

When you have diabetes, other health issues often tag along. These can include:

- heart disease
- high blood pressure
- kidney problems
- vision issues, like cataracts or glaucoma
- nerve damage (neuropathy)

These conditions can complicate diabetes management, but don't let that discourage you. With proper care and attention, many seniors successfully manage multiple health conditions.

MOBILITY LIMITATIONS

Staying active can become more challenging. Arthritis, balance issues, or diabetic neuropathy might make exercise seem daunting. However, physical activity remains important for managing blood sugar levels. Consider doing:

- chair exercises
- water aerobics
- gentle yoga or tai chi
- short, frequent walks

Any movement is better than none. Work with your doctor to find safe, enjoyable ways to stay active.

THE NEED FOR SOCIAL SUPPORT

Managing diabetes isn't a solo journey. Social support can make a big difference in how well you cope with the condition. This support can come from:

- family members
- friends
- support groups
- healthcare providers

Don't hesitate to reach out when you need help or just want to talk. Many communities offer diabetes support groups specifically for seniors.

PSYCHOLOGICAL IMPACT OF A DIABETES DIAGNOSIS

Learning you have diabetes can be overwhelming. It's normal to feel a range of emotions, including:

- shock or disbelief
- anger or frustration
- sadness or depression

- **anxiety about the future**

These feelings are valid, and it's important to acknowledge them. Don't allow them to keep you from taking the necessary steps to manage your health.

IMPORTANCE OF MENTAL HEALTH

Your mental well-being plays a crucial role in diabetes management. Stress, depression, and anxiety can affect your blood sugar levels and make it harder to stick to your care plan. To support your mental health:

- stay connected with your friends and family

- engage in activities you enjoy

- practice stress-reduction techniques like meditation or deep breathing

- seek professional help if you're struggling to cope

Don't hesitate to discuss your emotional well-being with your healthcare provider. They can offer resources or refer you to a mental health professional if needed.

Facing challenges doesn't mean you're failing at managing your diabetes. The key is to address these challenges head-on, with the support of your healthcare team and loved ones.

In the next sections, we'll explore strategies to overcome these hurdles and live well with diabetes.

*****

In **Chapter 2**, we'll explore the essential nutrients and foods that can help you manage diabetes effectively. We'll focus on practical dietary strategies, showing you how to make smart food choices that keep your blood sugar stable while still enjoying your meals.

2. ESSENTIAL NUTRIENTS AND FOODS FOR DIABETIC SENIORS

Managing diabetes effectively as a senior requires a solid understanding of key nutrients and their roles in your diet. This chapter aims to simplify the complex world of nutrition, helping you make informed food choices without feeling overwhelmed. We'll explore how different nutrients affect your blood sugar and overall health, and where to find them in your daily meals.

CARBOHYDRATES: THE ENERGY SOURCE

Carbohydrates are your body's primary energy source, but it's crucial to understand that not all carbs are created equal. **Simple carbohydrates,** found in foods like white bread, sugary drinks, and processed snacks, break down quickly in your body and **can cause rapid spikes in blood sugar**. On the other hand, **complex carbohydrates**, such as those in whole grains, beans, and most vegetables, take longer to digest, providing a more stable energy release and **gradual rise in blood sugar.**

For effective diabetes management, focus on incorporating more complex carbohydrates into your diet. These foods not only help maintain steadier blood sugar levels but also keep you feeling full for longer periods. When planning your meals, opt for whole grain products, legumes, and a variety of vegetables to ensure you're getting the right kind of carbohydrates for your health needs.

PROTEINS: BUILDING BLOCKS FOR HEALTH AND VITALITY

Protein plays a crucial role in maintaining muscle mass and overall health, which becomes increasingly important as we age. This essential nutrient helps build and repair tissues, create enzymes and hormones, and support immune function. For seniors managing diabetes, adequate **protein intake** is particularly vital for preserving **muscle mass**, aiding in wound healing, and promoting a feeling of fullness that can assist with weight management.

Incorporate protein into every meal to help stabilize your blood sugar and maintain satiety. Good sources of protein include animal-based options like lean meats (chicken, turkey, fish), eggs, and low-fat dairy, as well as plant-based alternatives such as beans, lentils, nuts, seeds, tofu, and tempeh. By varying your protein sources, you'll ensure a well-rounded nutrient intake while keeping your meals interesting and satisfying.

FATS: UNDERSTANDING THE GOOD AND THE BAD

Contrary to popular belief, not all fats are detrimental to your health. In fact, some fats are essential for maintaining good health, especially for seniors managing diabetes. The key is understanding the different types of fats and choosing the right ones. **Unsaturated fats**, including monounsaturated and polyunsaturated fats, offer numerous health benefits. They provide energy, help absorb certain vitamins, support brain function, and can even contribute to heart health by lowering bad cholesterol levels and reducing inflammation.

Focus on **incorporating healthy fats** into your diet through foods like avocados, nuts, seeds, olive oil, and fatty fish such as salmon. At the same time, aim to **reduce your intake of saturated fats** (found in animal products and some tropical oils) and **avoid trans fats** (artificially created fats) entirely. Simple changes, like choosing lean meats, using olive oil instead of butter, and limiting processed and fried foods, can significantly improve your fat intake profile and support your overall health goals.

FIBER: THE UNSUNG HERO OF DIABETES MANAGEMENT

Fiber is a powerhouse nutrient for managing diabetes and promoting overall digestive health. There are two types of fiber: soluble, which dissolves in water and helps control blood sugar, and insoluble, which aids in digestion. Both types offer significant benefits for diabetes management by **slowing digestion, preventing blood sugar spikes**, promoting a feeling of fullness, and even helping to lower cholesterol levels.

Aim to include a variety of high-fiber foods in your diet, such as whole grains, beans, lentils, fruits, vegetables (especially with the skin on), nuts, and seeds. Try adding a serving of vegetables to each meal, choosing whole grain bread and pasta, and snacking on fruits or nuts instead of processed foods. Gradually increase your fiber intake to reach the recommended 25-30 grams per day, being mindful to avoid digestive discomfort by making changes slowly (Dahl & Stewart, 2015.)

VITAMINS AND MINERALS: THE MICRONUTRIENT ESSENTIALS

While often overlooked, **vitamins** and **minerals** play crucial roles in your overall health and diabetes management. Key micronutrients for seniors with diabetes include Vitamin D, which helps your body use insulin effectively and supports bone health; Calcium, critical for bone health and potentially helpful in weight management; Magnesium, which aids in blood sugar regulation and heart health; and Potassium, important for managing blood pressure and supporting heart function.

To ensure you're getting enough of these essential micronutrients, focus on eating a varied diet rich in colorful fruits and vegetables, lean proteins, and whole grains. While supplements can be helpful, it's generally best to obtain nutrients from whole foods when possible, as your body typically absorbs and utilizes them more efficiently this way. If you're concerned about nutrient deficiencies, consult with your doctor about whether a multivitamin designed for seniors with diabetes might be beneficial for you.

Understanding and adding these essential nutrients into your daily diet can help you take significant steps toward effectively managing your diabetes and improving your overall health. Small, consistent changes in your eating habits can lead to substantial improvements in your well-being over time.

PUTTING KNOWLEDGE INTO PRACTICE: MEAL PLANNING AND PREPARATION

Understanding the role of various nutrients is just the first step in managing diabetes through diet. The next crucial phase is applying this knowledge to your daily meals. Let's explore some practical strategies for meal planning and preparation that can help you maintain stable blood sugar levels while enjoying delicious and nutritious food.

BALANCED PLATE METHOD

One of the simplest ways to ensure you're getting a good balance of nutrients is to use the "plate method." Visualize your plate divided into sections: half of it should be filled with non-starchy vegetables, a quarter with lean protein, and the remaining quarter with complex carbohydrates. This method naturally limits the amount of carbohydrates you consume while ensuring you get plenty of fiber, vitamins, and minerals from vegetables, along with satisfying protein.

A balanced dinner plate might include grilled chicken breast, quinoa, and a large serving of roasted broccoli and bell peppers. This combination provides a mix of protein, complex carbohydrates, and fiber-rich vegetables that will help keep your blood sugar stable and keep you feeling full.

PORTION CONTROL

As we age, our calorie needs often decrease, but the need for nutrients remains high. This makes **portion control** particularly important for seniors managing diabetes. Using smaller plates can help create the illusion of a full plate with less food.

Measuring tools like cups or a food scale can be helpful in the beginning to train your eye on appropriate portion sizes.

It's not only about eating less but about eating the right amounts of the right foods. A small portion of nuts, for instance, can be a nutrient-dense snack that helps stabilize blood sugar between meals.

MEAL PREPPING FOR CONSISTENCY

Consistency is key in managing diabetes, and **meal prepping can be an excellent tool** to achieve this. Dedicate some time each week to prepare several meals in advance. This not only ensures you have balanced meals ready when you're tired or short on time but also helps maintain consistent portion sizes and nutrient intake.

Try preparing a large batch of versatile protein like grilled chicken breasts, along with roasted vegetables and cooked quinoa. These can be mixed and matched throughout the week for varied meals that still meet your nutritional needs.

SMART SNACKING

Snacks can play an important role in managing blood sugar levels between meals. The key is choosing snacks that combine protein or healthy fats with complex carbohydrates. Some diabetes-friendly snack ideas include:

- Apple slices with a tablespoon of almond butter
- A small handful of nuts and a piece of cheese
- Carrot sticks with hummus
- Greek yogurt topped with berries and a sprinkle of granola

These snacks provide a good balance of nutrients to help keep you satisfied and maintain stable blood sugar levels.

HYDRATION IS KEY

While not a nutrient per se, proper **hydration is important** for your overall health and can impact blood sugar management. Thirst can be mistaken for hunger, leading to unnecessary snacking.

Keep a water bottle handy and aim to drink water regularly throughout the day. If you find plain water uninspiring, try infusing it with slices of lemon, cucumber, or berries for a refreshing twist.

MINDFUL EATING

Practicing **mindful eating** can help you better tune into your body's hunger and fullness cues, potentially improving your blood sugar management. Take time to savor your meals without distractions like television or phones. Pay attention to the flavors, textures, and sensations of eating. This can lead to greater satisfaction with smaller portions and help prevent overeating.

ADAPTING RECIPES

You don't have to give up your favorite foods to manage diabetes. Many recipes can be adapted to be more diabetes-friendly. For instance:

- **Replace refined grains with whole grains** (e.g., whole wheat pasta instead of white pasta)
- **Reduce the amount of added sugars** in recipes, or use natural sweeteners like fruit purees
- **Increase the proportion of vegetables in dishes**
- **Use healthy cooking methods** like grilling, roasting, or steaming instead of frying

Managing diabetes through diet doesn't mean a life of restriction. It's about making informed choices and finding a balance that works for you.

By applying the principles we've discussed about nutrients and implementing these practical strategies, you can create a sustainable, enjoyable eating plan that supports your health goals.

*****

In the next chapter, we'll explore how creating a balanced meal plan can complement your nutrition efforts in managing diabetes.

3. CREATING A BALANCED MEAL PLAN

This chapter is all about putting your nutrition knowledge into action. We'll cover how to plan meals that keep your blood sugar stable and your taste buds happy.

THE BASICS OF MEAL PLANNING

Meal planning isn't only about what you eat, but when and how much. This comprehensive approach to nutrition is crucial for maintaining overall health and well-being.

IMPORTANCE OF MEAL PLANNING

Effective meal planning **helps maintain stable blood sugar levels**, ensures balanced nutrition, and can save both time and money. It also significantly reduces stress around food choices, making it easier to maintain a healthy diet.

BALANCING MACRONUTRIENTS

When planning your meals, aim for a mix of carbs, proteins, and fats at each sitting. A general guideline is to fill half your plate with non-starchy vegetables, a quarter with protein, and the remaining quarter with complex carbohydrates. This balance helps ensure you're getting a wide range of nutrients.

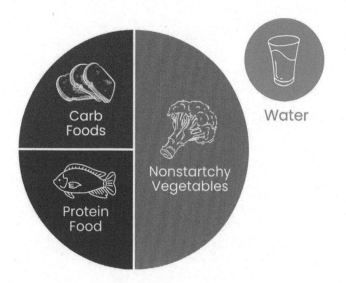

PORTION CONTROL

Use the plate method mentioned above as a guide for portion sizes. Consider using smaller plates to naturally reduce portions. It's worth noting that portion sizes often decrease as we age due to lower calorie needs, so be mindful of adjusting your intake accordingly.

TIMING OF MEALS

Aim for **regular meal times** to help stabilize blood sugar. Some people find that eating smaller, more frequent meals works better for them. Regardless of your preferred eating schedule, it's important not to skip meals, especially breakfast, as this can disrupt your metabolism and energy levels.

PRACTICAL TIPS

To make meal planning more manageable, try planning your meals a week in advance. Cooking in batches and freezing portions for later can save time on busy days. Keep a well-stocked pantry with healthy staples to make impromptu meal preparation easier. These strategies can help you maintain a consistent and nutritious eating plan.

SAMPLE WEEKLY MEAL PLAN

Here's a basic outline for a week of balanced meals. We'll provide more detailed recipes later in the book.

Day	Meal	Recipe	Page
Monday	Breakfast	Overnight steel-cut oats	31
	Snack	Almond flour raspberry muffin	56
	Lunch	Grilled chicken and vegetable wrap	36
	Snack	Homemade hummus with vegetable crudités	49
	Dinner	Baked cod with vegetables, lemon, and herbs	42
Tuesday	Breakfast	Greek yogurt parfait with berries and nuts	30
	Snack	Baked zucchini chips	49
	Lunch	Turkey and avocado lettuce	37
	Snack	Low-GI seed and nut bar	48
	Dinner	Grilled lean steak with roasted asparagus and tomatoes	43
Thursday	Breakfast	Avocado toast on whole-grain bread	31
	Snack	Roasted chickpea snack mix	52
	Lunch	Lentil soup with whole grain crackers	37
	Snack	Greek yogurt bark with berries and nuts	50
	Dinner	Stuffed bell peppers with ground turkey and quinoa	45
Thursday	Breakfast	Veggie and cheese omelet	30
	Snack	Chia seed pudding snack cups	48
	Lunch	Tuna salad on a bed of leafy greens	23
	Snack	Almond flour crackers	50
	Dinner	Shrimp and broccoli stir-fry	44

Day	Meal	Recipe	Page
Friday	Breakfast	Protein smoothie	33
	Snack	Baked sweet potato fries	51
	Lunch	Chickpea and spinach curry	46
	Snack	Avocado and black bean dip	51
	Dinner	Vegetarian chili with mixed beans	44
Saturday	Breakfast	Cottage cheese with cinnamon and berries	34
	Snack	Flaxseed and almond meal muffins	52
	Lunch	Zucchini noodles with lean turkey meatballs	40
	Snack	Low-GI seed and nut bars	48
	Dinner	Baked eggplant parmesan	45
	Dessert	Sugar-free peanut butter cups (optional)	56
Sunday	Breakfast	Baked Egg Cups	34
	Snack	Grilled peaches with ricotta and honey	57
	Lunch	Mediterranean chickpea salad	39
	Snack	Almond flour crackers	50
	Dinner	Grilled pork tenderloin with roasted sweet potatoes	45
	Dessert	Sugar-free chocolate avocado mousse (optional)	54

This meal plan combines a variety of nutrients, balances carbohydrates, proteins, and healthy fats, and includes plenty of fiber-rich foods. Adjust portion sizes as needed.

SCAN THE QR CODE BELOW TO ACCESS AND DOWNLOAD OUR COMPREHENSIVE GROCERY LIST AND IDENTIFY THE BEST LOW-GI OPTIONS FOR YOUR SHOPPING CART.

TIPS FOR GROCERY SHOPPING

Smart grocery shopping is key to managing diabetes. Let's discuss how to make the most of your trips to the store.

READING FOOD LABELS

When examining food labels, start by checking serving sizes to understand the nutritional information in context. **Look at total carbohydrates, not just sugar,** as all carbs affect blood glucose.

Choose foods with higher fiber content, which can help manage blood sugar levels. Aim for **lower sodium** options to support heart health.

Be wary of "sugar-free" labels, as these products may still contain carbs that can affect blood sugar.

MAKING HEALTHY CHOICES

To make healthier choices, focus on shopping the perimeter of the store where fresh foods are usually located. Choose whole fruits over fruit juices to benefit from added fiber.

Opt for **lean meats** and fish as protein sources. When it comes to grains, select **whole grain** options over refined grains for better nutrition and blood sugar management. Don't forget to pick up plenty of **non-starchy vegetables**, which are low in carbs and high in nutrients.

COMMON PITFALLS TO AVOID

There are several pitfalls to be aware of when grocery shopping. Don't shop when you're hungry, as this can lead to impulsive, less healthy choices. Be cautious of "health food" claims and always check the label for accurate nutritional information.

Watch out for hidden sugars in sauces and dressings, which can add unexpected carbs to your meals. Also, don't assume all organic foods are low in carbs or calories - they can still impact blood sugar levels.

GROCERY LIST SUGGESTIONS

When creating your grocery list, focus on nutrient-dense foods from various food groups. For produce, include leafy greens, non-starchy vegetables, and low-glycemic fruits.

In the protein section, opt for lean meats, fish, eggs, and plant-based options like tofu.

For dairy, choose low-fat milk, yogurt, and cheese. When selecting grains, prioritize whole-grain bread, brown rice, and quinoa.

Don't forget to include sources of healthy fats such as olive oil, avocados, nuts, and seeds. This balanced approach to shopping can help you maintain a diabetes-friendly diet.

ADJUSTING MEAL PLANS FOR SPECIAL OCCASIONS

Special occasions don't have to derail your diabetes management. Let's find out how to navigate them.

Diabetic seniors often face several challenges during special occasions. These challenges can include some of the following:

- The temptation of high-carb, high-sugar foods can be overwhelming, potentially leading to blood sugar spikes.
- Pressure from family or friends to indulge in traditional dishes may create social discomfort.
- Estimating the carbohydrate content of unfamiliar foods can be difficult, making it challenging to maintain proper glucose control.

TIPS FOR HOLIDAYS

During holidays, it's important to maintain a **balanced approach**. Don't skip meals to "save" calories for later, as this can lead to overeating and blood sugar fluctuations. Instead, consider bringing a diabetes-friendly dish to share, ensuring you have a healthy option available. When filling your plate, aim to make half of it vegetables to help control carbohydrate intake. It's okay to enjoy small portions of treats, savoring them mindfully without overindulging.

FOR FAMILY GATHERINGS

Family gatherings can be navigated successfully with some preparation. **Communicate your dietary needs** to the host in advance, allowing them to accommodate your requirements. Offering to help with meal planning or preparation gives you more control over the menu. Remember to focus on socializing and enjoying the company of loved ones, rather than centering the gathering solely around food.

DINING OUT

When dining out, a little forethought goes a long way. If possible, review the menu online beforehand to identify diabetes-friendly options. When ordering, ask for sauces and dressings on the side to control added sugars and fats. Opt for grilled or baked dishes instead of fried ones to reduce unnecessary carbohydrates and calories. Don't hesitate to ask how dishes are prepared – this information can help you make informed choices that align with your diabetes management plan.

MANAGING BLOOD SUGAR DURING SPECIAL OCCASIONS

Life is full of celebrations and special events, and having diabetes doesn't mean you have to miss out on the joy these occasions bring. With thoughtful planning and smart strategies, you can participate fully in festivities while keeping your blood sugar levels in check.

The key is finding a balance between enjoying yourself and maintaining your health goals, ensuring that special days don't derail your overall diabetes management efforts.

- **Test your blood sugar** more frequently
- **Stay hydrated** with water
- **Take a walk** after meals to help lower blood sugar
- **Adjust medication** as advised by your doctor

It's okay to enjoy special occasions. The key is **moderation** and **planning.** If you slip up, don't beat yourself up—just get back on track with your next meal.

For more detailed guidance on navigating special occasions while managing your diabetes, check out our free ebook *Festive Feasts: Diabetes-Friendly Recipes for Special Occasions.*

This resource provides a variety of **low-GI recipes** and menu plans designed specifically for celebrations, helping you enjoy special moments without compromising your health.

*****

Now, the most exciting part is here! **In the next chapter** let's explore healthy and tasty recipes.

4. DELICIOUS AND EASY RECIPES

In this chapter, you will explore a variety of delicious and easy-to-prepare recipes that are ideal for diabetic seniors. These recipes show us that managing diabetes doesn't mean sacrificing flavor or enjoyment in meals. Included in the chapter are recipes for breakfast, lunch, dinner, snacks, desserts, and quick meals for busy days. Each recipe is designed to be nutritious, easy to follow, and adaptable to individual tastes and dietary needs.

BREAKFAST

et's explore healthy and tasty breakfast recipes that are easy to prepare and perfect for starting
our day off right.

GREEK YOGURT PARFAIT WITH BERRIES AND NUTS

NUTRITIONAL VALUES (PER SERVING)
Calories: 185 *Carbohydrates:* 15g *Fiber:* 3g *Sugars:* 9g *Protein:* 14g *Fat:* 9g

PREP TIME
10 minutes

COOK TIME
0 minutes

SERVINGS
4

Storage Tip: These parfaits are best consumed fresh. However, you can prepare the components separately and store them in airtight containers in the refrigerator. The yogurt mixture will keep for up to 3 days, and the chopped nuts can be stored at room temperature for up to a week. Assemble just before serving.

INGREDIENTS

- 2 cups (500g) plain, non-fat Greek yogurt
- 1 cup (150g) mixed berries (strawberries, blueberries, raspberries)
- 1/4 cup (30g) chopped almonds
- 1/4 cup (30g) chopped walnuts
- 1 teaspoon (5ml) vanilla extract
- 1/4 teaspoon (1g) ground cinnamon
- 4 teaspoons (20ml) sugar-free maple syrup (optional)

INSTRUCTIONS

1. In a small bowl, mix the Greek yogurt with vanilla extract and cinnamon until well combined.
2. If using larger berries like strawberries, chop them into bite-sized pieces.
3. In four serving glasses or bowls, begin layering the parfait:
4. Start with 1/4 cup of the yogurt mixture in each glass
5. Add 2 tablespoons of mixed berries on top of the yogurt
6. Sprinkle 1 tablespoon of the mixed chopped nuts over the berries
7. Repeat the layering process one more time in each glass.
8. If desired, drizzle 1 teaspoon of sugar-free maple syrup over each parfait.
9. Serve immediately, or cover with plastic wrap and refrigerate for up 2 hours before serving.

VEGGIE AND CHEESE OMELET

NUTRITIONAL VALUES (PER SERVING)

Calories: 165 *Carbohydrates:* 6g *Fiber:* 2g *Sugars:* 3g *Protein:* 14g *Fat:* 10g

Storage Tip: Cooked omelets can be stored in an airtight container in the refrigerator for up to 2 days. Reheat in a microwave or a skillet over low heat

PREP TIME
10 minutes

COOK TIME
8 minutes

SERVINGS
4

INGREDIENTS

- 8 large eggs
- 4 tablespoons (60ml) water
- 1 teaspoon (1g) dried oregano
- 1/2 teaspoon (3g) salt
- 1/4 teaspoon (0.5g) ground black pepper
- 1 cup (150g) cherry tomatoes, halved
- 1 cup (100g) bell peppers, diced
- 1 cup (30g) baby spinach leaves
- 1/2 cup (56g) reduced-fat cheddar cheese, shredded
- Nonstick cooking spray
- 2 tablespoons (8g) fresh chives, chopped (for garnish)

INSTRUCTIONS

1. In a medium bowl, whisk together eggs, water, oregano, salt, and pepper until well combined.
2. In a separate bowl, mix together tomatoes, bell peppers, and spinach
3. Coat a 10-inch (25cm) nonstick skillet with cooking spray and heat over medium heat.
4. For each omelet: a. Pour 1/2 cup (120ml) of the egg mixture into the skillet. b. Cook, gently pushing the edges toward the center with a spatula as they set, allowing uncooked egg to flow underneath. c. When the egg is mostly set but still slightly wet on top, spread 1/4 of the vegetable mixture over half of the omelet. d. Sprinkle 2 tablespoons of cheese over the vegetables. e. Using a spatula, fold the other half of the omelet over the filling. f. Cook for another 1-2 minu until the cheese melts and the omelet is golden brown on the bott
5. Carefully slide the omelet onto a plate and garnish with fresh chive
6. Repeat the process to make 4 omelets total, wiping the skillet clear and respraying with cooking spray between each omelet.
7. Serve hot.

OVERNIGHT STEEL-CUT OATS

NUTRITIONAL VALUES (PER SERVING)
Calories: 220 *Carbohydrates:* 32g *Fiber:* 5g *Sugars:* 4g *Protein:* 8g *Fat:* 7g

PREP TIME
10 minutes

COOK TIME
8 hours soaking

SERVINGS
4 (1 cup)

Storage Tip: The prepared oat mixture (without toppings) can be stored in an airtight container in the refrigerator for up to 5 days. Add fresh toppings just before serving.

INGREDIENTS

- 1 cup (180g) steel-cut oats
- 2 cups (480ml) unsweetened almond milk
- 1 cup (240ml) water
- 2 tablespoons (30ml) chia seeds
- 1 teaspoon (5ml) vanilla extract
- 1/2 teaspoon (2.5g) ground cinnamon
- 1/4 teaspoon (1.25g) salt
- 1/4 cup (30g) chopped walnuts
- 1 medium apple, diced (about 1 cup or 125g)
- 4 teaspoons (20ml) sugar-free maple syrup (optional, for serving)
- sugar-free chocolate chips for decoration (optional)

INSTRUCTIONS

1. In a large glass or plastic container with a lid, combine the steel-cut oats, almond milk, water, chia seeds, vanilla extract, cinnamon, and salt. Stir well to combine.
2. Cover the container and refrigerate overnight or for at least 8 hours.
3. In the morning, stir the oat mixture. If it's too thick, add a little more almond milk to reach your desired consistency.
4. Divide the oat mixture evenly among 4 bowls.
5. Top each bowl with 1 tablespoon of chopped walnuts and 1/4 cup of diced apple.
6. If desired, drizzle 1 teaspoon of sugar-free maple syrup over each serving.
7. Serve cold, or heat in the microwave for 1-2 minutes if you prefer warm oatmeal.

AVOCADO TOAST ON WHOLE-GRAIN BREAD

NUTRITIONAL VALUES (PER SERVING)
Calories: 195 *Carbohydrates:* 20g *Fiber:* 7g *Sugars:* 2g *Protein:* 6g *Fat:* 12g

Storage Tip: This dish is best prepared and eaten fresh. If needed, you can store the mashed avocado mixture separately in an airtight container with plastic wrap pressed directly onto the surface to prevent browning. Refrigerate for up to 1 day. Assemble the toast just before serving.

PREP TIME
10 minutes

COOK TIME
5 minutes

SERVINGS
4

INGREDIENTS

- 4 slices whole-grain bread (about 30g each)
- 2 medium ripe avocados (about 200g total)
- 1 tablespoon (15ml) fresh lemon juice
- 1/4 teaspoon (1.5g) salt
- 1/4 teaspoon (0.5g) black pepper
- 1/2 cup (75g) cherry tomatoes, quartered
- 2 tablespoons (10g) red onion, finely diced
- 2 tablespoons (8g) fresh cilantro, chopped
- 1/4 teaspoon (0.5g) red pepper flakes (optional)

INSTRUCTIONS

1. Toast the whole-grain bread slices until golden brown and crispy.
2. While the bread is toasting, cut the avocados in half, remove the pit, and scoop the flesh into a medium bowl.
3. Add lemon juice, salt, and black pepper to the avocado. Mash with a fork until mostly smooth, leaving some small chunks for texture.
4. In a separate small bowl, mix together the quartered cherry tomatoes, diced red onion, and chopped cilantro.
5. Spread the mashed avocado evenly over each slice of toasted bread (about 1/4 of the mixture per slice).
6. Top each toast with an equal amount of the tomato-onion-cilantro mixture.
7. If desired, sprinkle red pepper flakes over the top for an extra kick.
8. Serve immediately.

CHIA SEED BREAKFAST TREAT

NUTRITIONAL VALUES (PER SERVING)

Calories: 165 *Carbohydrates:* 14g *Fiber:* 10g *Sugars:* 2g *Protein:* 6g *Fat:* 11g

PREP TIME
11
minutes

COOK TIME
4
hours chilling

SERVINGS
4 (120ml)

Storage Tip: The prepared chia seed pudding (without toppings) can be stored in an airtight container in the refrigerator for up to 5 days. Add fresh toppings just before serving.

INGREDIENTS

- 1/2 cup (80g) chia seeds
- 2 cups (480ml) unsweetened almond milk
- 1 teaspoon (5ml) vanilla extract
- 1/4 teaspoon (1.25g) ground cinnamon
- 2 tablespoons (30ml) sugar-free maple syrup (optional)
- 1 cup (150g) mixed berries (strawberries, blueberries, raspberries)
- 1/4 cup (30g) sliced almonds

INSTRUCTIONS

1. In a medium bowl, whisk together chia seeds, almond milk, vanilla extract, cinnamon, and sugar-free maple syrup (if using) until well combined.
2. Cover the bowl with plastic wrap or transfer the mixture to an airtight container.
3. Refrigerate for at least 4 hours or overnight, until the mixture has thickened to a pudding-like consistency.
4. After chilling, stir the pudding well to break up any clumps.
5. Divide the chia seed pudding evenly among 4 serving bowls or glasses.
6. Top each serving with 1/4 cup of mixed berries and 1 tablespoon of sliced almonds.
7. Serve chilled.

VEGETABLE FRITTATA

NUTRITIONAL VALUES (PER SERVING)

Calories: 180 *Carbohydrates:* 6g *Fiber:* 2g *Sugars:* 3g *Protein:* 14g *Fat:* 12g

Storage Tip: Leftover frittata can be stored in an airtight container in the refrigerator for up to 3 days. Reheat individual slices in the microwave for 30-45 seconds, or until warmed through.

PREP TIME
15
minutes

COOK TIME
25
minutes

SERVINGS
6
(1/6 of frittata)

INGREDIENTS

- 8 large eggs
- 1/4 cup (60ml) unsweetened almond milk
- 1/2 teaspoon (3g) salt
- 1/4 teaspoon (0.5g) black pepper
- 1 tablespoon (15ml) olive oil
- 1 small onion, diced (about 1 cup or 150g)
- 1 red bell pepper, diced (about 1 cup or 150g)
- 2 cups (60g) baby spinach
- 1 cup (150g) cherry tomatoes, halved
- 1/2 cup (56g) reduced-fat feta cheese, crumbled
- 2 tablespoons (8g) fresh basil, chopped
- Nonstick cooking spray

INSTRUCTIONS

1. Preheat the oven to 375°F (190°C).
2. In a large bowl, whisk together eggs, almond milk, salt, and pepper until well combined. Set aside.
3. Heat olive oil in a 10-inch (25cm) oven-safe nonstick skillet over medium heat.
4. Add onion and bell pepper to the skillet. Cook, stirring occasionally, until softened, about 5-7 minutes.
5. Add spinach to the skillet and cook until wilted about 2 minutes.
6. Spread the vegetables evenly in the skillet. Pour the egg mixture over the vegetables.
7. Sprinkle cherry tomatoes and crumbled feta cheese over the top.
8. Cook on the stovetop for 3-4 minutes, until the edges start to set.
9. Transfer the skillet to the preheated oven and bake for 15-18 minutes or until the frittata is set and lightly golden on top.
10. Remove from the oven and let cool for 5 minutes.
11. Sprinkle chopped basil over the top.
12. Slice into 6 wedges and serve.

PROTEIN SMOOTHIE

NUTRITIONAL VALUES (PER SERVING)
Calories: 210 *Carbohydrates:* 18g *Fiber:* 6g *Sugars:* 8g *Protein:* 20g *Fat:* 8g

PREP TIME
5
minutes

COOK TIME
0
minutes

SERVINGS
2 (1 cup)

Storage Tip: This smoothie is best consumed immediately after blending. If needed, you can store it in an airtight container in the refrigerator for up to 24 hours. Shake or stir well before drinking.

INGREDIENTS

- cup (240ml) unsweetened almond milk
- scoop (30g) unsweetened whey protein powder (or plant-based protein powder)
- /2 medium avocado (about 75g)
- cup (30g) fresh spinach or kale leaves
- /2 cup (75g) frozen mixed berries (strawberries, blueberries, raspberries)
- tablespoon (15g) chia seeds
- /2 teaspoon (2.5ml) vanilla extract
- /2 cup (120ml) water
- 4-5 ice cubes

INSTRUCTIONS

1. Add all ingredients to a blender in the order listed.
2. Blend on high speed for 30-60 seconds, or until smooth and creamy.
3. If the smoothie is too thick, add a little more water or almond milk and blend again.
4. Taste and adjust sweetness if needed by adding a small amount of stevia or another sugar-free sweetener.
5. Pour into two glasses and serve immediately.

SAVORY BREAKFAST BOWL

NUTRITIONAL VALUES (PER SERVING)
Calories: 320 *Carbohydrates:* 20g *Fiber:* 7g *Sugars:* 3g *Protein:* 24g *Fat:* 18g

Storage Tip: This bowl is best assembled fresh. You can prep components ahead of time: Cook quinoa and store in an airtight container in the refrigerator for up to 3 days; Sauté vegetables and store separately for up to 2 days; Soft-boil eggs and store unpeeled in the refrigerator for up to 2 days.

PREP TIME
10
minutes

COOK TIME
15
minutes

SERVINGS
2
(1 bowl)

INGREDIENTS

- /2 cup (90g) quinoa, rinsed
- cup (240ml) water
- large eggs
- tablespoon (15ml) olive oil
- cup (100g) cherry tomatoes, halved
- cups (60g) baby spinach
- /4 cup (40g) red onion, finely chopped
- cup (100g) mushrooms, sliced
- cup (100g) cucumber, sliced
- tablespoons (30g) feta cheese, crumbled
- tablespoons (30ml) plain Greek yogurt (optional)
- tablespoon (4g) parsley or fresh chives, chopped
- alt and pepper to taste
- ot sauce (optional, for serving)

INSTRUCTIONS

1. In a small saucepan, combine quinoa and water. Bring to a boil, then reduce heat to low, cover, and simmer for about 15 minutes or until water is absorbed and quinoa is fluffy.
2. While quinoa is cooking, bring another small pot of water to a boil. Carefully add the eggs and cook for 6-7 minutes for soft-boiled eggs. Remove eggs and place in an ice bath to stop cooking.
3. Heat olive oil in a skillet over medium heat. Add cherry tomatoes and red onion, cooking for about 3-4 minutes until tomatoes start to soften.
4. Add spinach to the skillet and cook until just wilted, about 1-2 minutes.
5. Divide the cooked quinoa between two bowls.
6. Top each bowl with the sautéed vegetables, dividing them equally.
7. Peel the eggs and cut them in half. Place one egg (two halves) on top of each bowl.
8. Add sliced avocado, cucumbers, mushrooms, and crumbled feta cheese to each bowl.
9. Dollop 1 tablespoon of Greek yogurt onto each bowl (if you prefer).
10. Sprinkle with chopped chives and season with salt and pepper to taste.
11. Serve immediately, with hot sauce on the side if desired.

COTTAGE CHEESE WITH CINNAMON AND BERRIES

NUTRITIONAL VALUES (PER SERVING)
Calories: 220 *Carbohydrates:* 8g *Fiber:* 3g *Sugars:* 4g *Protein:* 25g *Fat:* 11g

PREP TIME
5
minutes

COOK TIME
0
minutes

SERVINGS
2
(1 cup)

Storage Tip: This dish is best prepared fresh. You can store the plain cottage cheese in an airtight container in the refrigerator for up to 5 days. Add the toppings just before serving to maintain their texture.

INGREDIENTS

- 2 cups (480g) low-fat cottage cheese (1% milk fat)
- 1 teaspoon (2g) ground cinnamon
- 1/4 cup (40g) fresh berries (strawberries, blueberries, or raspberries)
- 1/4 cup (30g) mixed chopped nuts (optional)
- 1 teaspoon (5ml) vanilla extract
- 2 teaspoons (10ml) sugar-free maple syrup (optional)

INSTRUCTIONS

1. In a medium bowl, combine the cottage cheese and vanilla extract. Mix well.
2. Divide the cottage cheese mixture evenly between two serving bowls.
3. Sprinkle 1/2 teaspoon of ground cinnamon over each bowl of cottage cheese.
4. Top each bowl with 2 tablespoons of the chopped mixed nuts.
5. Add 2 tablespoons of fresh berries to each bowl.
6. If desired, drizzle 1 teaspoon of sugar-free maple syrup over each serving for added sweetness.
7. Serve immediately.

BAKED EGG CUPS

NUTRITIONAL VALUES (PER SERVING)

Calories: 180 *Carbohydrates:* 4g *Fiber:* 1g *Sugars:* 2g *Protein:* 14g *Fat:* 13g

Storage Tip: These egg cups can be stored in an airtight container in the refrigerator for up to 4 days. To reheat, microwave for 30-45 seconds or until warmed through. They can also be frozen for up to 2 months. Thaw overnight in the refrigerator before reheating.

PREP TIME
15
minutes

COOK TIME
20
minutes

SERVINGS
6
(2 egg cups)

INGREDIENTS

- 12 large eggs
- 1/4 cup (60ml) unsweetened almond milk
- 1/2 teaspoon (3g) salt
- 1/4 teaspoon (0.5g) black pepper
- 1 cup (150g) mixed vegetables, finely chopped (like bell peppers, spinach, onions)
- 1/2 cup (56g) reduced-fat cheddar cheese, shredded
- 2 tablespoons (8g) fresh chives, chopped
- Non-stick cooking spray

INSTRUCTIONS

1. Preheat the oven to 350ºF (175ºC).
2. Lightly grease a 12-cup muffin tin with non-stick cooking spray.
3. In a large bowl, whisk together eggs, almond milk, salt, and pepper until well combined.
4. Evenly distribute the chopped vegetables among the muffin cups.
5. Pour the egg mixture over the vegetables, filling each cup about 3/4 full.
6. Sprinkle shredded cheese evenly over each cup.
7. Bake for 18-20 minutes, or until the eggs are set and slightly golden on top.
8. Remove from the oven and let cool in the tin for 5 minutes.
9. Carefully remove the egg cups from the tin using a knife or spatula loosen the edges.
10. Sprinkle chopped chives over the top before serving.

LUNCH

Let's explore healthy and tasty lunch recipes that are easy to prepare and perfect energy sources for getting through the rest of your day.

QUINOA AND BLACK BEAN SALAD

NUTRITIONAL VALUES (PER SERVING)

Calories: 250 *Carbohydrates:* 40g *Fiber:* 10g *Sugars:* 3g *Protein:* 12g *Fat:* 7g

PREP TIME
15 minutes

COOK TIME
15 minutes

SERVINGS
4 (1 cup)

Storage Tip: This salad can be stored in an airtight container in the refrigerator for up to 3 days. If preparing in advance, add the avocado just before serving to prevent browning.

INGREDIENTS

- 1 cup (170g) quinoa, rinsed
- 2 cups (480ml) water
- 1 can (15 oz/425g) black beans or kidney beans, drained and rinsed
- 1 cup (150g) cherry tomatoes, halved
- 1 small red bell pepper, diced
- 1/2 red onion, finely chopped
- 1/2 cup (8g) fresh cilantro, chopped
- 1 avocado, diced (optional)

For the dressing:
- 3 tablespoons (45ml) lime juice
- 2 tablespoons (30ml) extra-virgin olive oil
- 1 clove garlic, minced
- 1 teaspoon (2g) ground cumin
- 1/4 teaspoon (1.5g) salt
- 1/4 teaspoon (0.5g) black pepper

INSTRUCTIONS

1. In a medium saucepan, combine quinoa and water. Bring to a boil, then reduce heat to low, cover, and simmer for about 15 minutes or until water is absorbed and quinoa is fluffy.
2. Transfer the cooked quinoa to a large bowl and let it cool to room temperature.
3. While the quinoa is cooling, prepare the dressing. In a small bowl, whisk together lime juice, olive oil, minced garlic, cumin, salt, and pepper.
4. Once the quinoa has cooled, add black beans, cherry tomatoes, diced bell pepper, red onion, and cilantro to the bowl.
5. Pour the dressing over the salad and gently toss to combine all ingredients.
6. Just before serving, add the diced avocado and gently fold it into the salad.
7. Taste and adjust seasoning if necessary.
8. Serve chilled or at room temperature.

GRILLED CHICKEN AND VEGETABLE WRAP

NUTRITIONAL VALUES (PER SERVING)

Calories: 310 *Carbohydrates:* 25g *Fiber:* 8g *Sugars:* 3g *Protein:* 28g *Fat:* 12g

Storage Tip: These wraps are best enjoyed fresh. You can grill the chicken and vegetables in advance and store them separately in airtight containers in the refrigerator for up to 3 days. Assemble the wraps just before serving.

PREP TIME
15 minutes

COOK TIME
15 minutes

SERVINGS
4 (1 wrap)

INGREDIENTS

- 4 low-carb, high-fiber whole wheat tortillas (8-inch diameter)
- 16 oz (450g) boneless, skinless chicken breast (replace with tofu for a non-meat option)
- 2 tablespoons (30ml) olive oil, divided
- 1 teaspoon (2g) dried oregano
- 1/2 teaspoon (1g) garlic powder
- 1/4 teaspoon (1.5g) salt
- 1/4 teaspoon (0.5g) black pepper
- 1 medium zucchini, sliced lengthwise
- 1 red bell pepper, sliced
- 1 small red onion, sliced
- 4 tablespoons (60g) hummus
- 2 cups (60g) mixed salad greens

For the yogurt sauce:
- 1/2 cup (120g) plain Greek yogurt
- 1 tablespoon (15ml) lemon juice
- 1 clove garlic, minced
- 1 tablespoon (4g) fresh dill, chopped
- Salt and pepper to taste

INSTRUCTIONS

1. In a small bowl, mix 1 tablespoon olive oil with oregano, garlic powder, salt, and black pepper. Rub this mixture over the chicken breasts.
2. Preheat a grill or grill pan over medium-high heat. Grill the chicken for 6-7 minutes per side, or until fully cooked (internal temperature of 165°F/74°C). Set aside to rest for 5 minutes, then slice.
3. While the chicken is cooking, toss zucchini, bell pepper, and onion with the remaining 1 tablespoon of olive oil. Grill the vegetables for 3-4 minutes per side, until tender and lightly charred.
4. Prepare the yogurt sauce by mixing all sauce ingredients in a small bowl.
5. To assemble the wraps, spread 1 tablespoon of hummus on each tortilla.
6. Layer each tortilla with 1/2 cup of mixed greens, 1/4 of the grilled vegetables, and 1/4 of the sliced chicken.
7. Drizzle 2 tablespoons of the yogurt sauce over each wrap.
8. Fold in the sides of the tortilla and roll tightly to enclose the filling.
9. Cut each wrap in half diagonally and serve immediately.

LENTIL SOUP WITH WHOLE GRAIN CRACKERS

NUTRITIONAL VALUES (PER SERVING)

Calories: 280 *Carbohydrates:* 45g *Fiber:* 16g *Sugars:* 5g *Protein:* 16g *Fat:* 5g

PREP TIME	COOK TIME	SERVINGS
15 minutes	35 minutes	6

Storage Tip: This soup can be stored in an airtight container in the refrigerator for up to 4 days, or frozen for up to 3 months. Reheat gently on the stovetop or in the microwave. Store crackers separately to maintain their crispness.

INGREDIENTS

Lentil Soup:

- tablespoon (15ml) olive oil
- large onion, diced
- celery stalks, chopped
- medium carrots, diced
- cloves garlic, minced
- cup (200g) dry brown lentils, rinsed and picked over
- can (14.5 oz/411g) diced tomatoes, no salt added
- cups (1.4L) low-sodium vegetable broth
- bay leaves
- teaspoon (2g) ground cumin
- teaspoon (2g) dried thyme
- 4 teaspoon (0.5g) black pepper
- cups (60g) fresh spinach, chopped
- tablespoons (30ml) lemon juice
- fresh parsley (for garnish)
- salt to taste (optional)

For serving:

- 24 whole-grain crackers (about 60g total, choose a low-sodium variety)

INSTRUCTIONS

1. Heat olive oil in a large pot over medium heat. Add onion, celery, and carrots. Cook for 5-7 minutes until vegetables start to soften.
2. Add garlic and cook for another minute until fragrant.
3. Stir in lentils, diced tomatoes, vegetable broth, bay leaves, cumin, thyme, and black pepper. Bring to a boil.
4. Reduce heat, cover, and simmer for about 25-30 minutes, or until lentils are tender.
5. Remove bay leaves. Use an immersion blender to partially blend the soup, leaving some chunks for texture. Alternatively, blend about 2 cups of the soup in a regular blender and return it to the pot.
6. Stir in chopped spinach and lemon juice. Cook for an additional 2-3 minutes until spinach is wilted.
7. Taste and adjust seasoning if needed. Add salt if desired, but keep in mind the crackers may add saltiness.
8. Garnish with fresh parsley.
9. Serve hot with 4 whole grain crackers per serving.

TURKEY AND AVOCADO LETTUCE WRAPS

NUTRITIONAL VALUES (PER SERVING)

Calories: 240 *Carbohydrates:* 8g *Fiber:* 5g *Sugars:* 2g *Protein:* 25g *Fat:* 14g

Storage Tip: These wraps are best assembled just before eating to keep the lettuce crisp. However, you can prep all the ingredients separately and store them in airtight containers in the refrigerator for up to 2 days. Assemble the wraps when ready to eat.

PREP TIME	COOK TIME	SERVINGS
15 minutes	0 minutes	4 (2 lettuce wraps)

INGREDIENTS

- large lettuce leaves (Boston, Bibb, or Romaine)
- oz (340g) sliced turkey breast, low-sodium
- large avocado, sliced
- medium carrot, diced
- 4 red onion, thinly sliced
- 2 cucumber, sliced into thin strips
- tablespoons (30ml) Dijon mustard
- tablespoons (30g) plain Greek yogurt
- tablespoon (15ml) lemon juice
- 4 teaspoon (0.5g) black pepper
- *Optional*: 1/4 cup (10g) fresh herbs (e.g., cilantro, basil, or parsley), chopped

INSTRUCTIONS

1. Wash and dry the lettuce leaves carefully, ensuring they remain intact.
2. In a small bowl, mix together Dijon mustard, Greek yogurt, lemon juice, and black pepper to create the dressing.
3. Lay out the lettuce leaves on a clean surface.
4. Divide the sliced turkey breast evenly among the lettuce leaves.
5. Top each wrap with sliced avocado, diced tomato, red onion slices, and cucumber strips.
6. Drizzle about 1 tablespoon of the dressing over each wrap.
7. If using, sprinkle chopped fresh herbs over the fillings.
8. Carefully roll up each lettuce leaf, tucking in the sides as you go, to form a wrap.
9. Secure each wrap with a toothpick if needed.
10. Serve immediately.

BAKED SALMON WITH ROASTED VEGETABLES

NUTRITIONAL VALUES (PER SERVING)

Calories: 320 *Carbohydrates:* 15g *Fiber:* 5g *Sugars:* 6g *Protein:* 28g *Fat:* 18g

PREP TIME	COOK TIME	SERVINGS
15 minutes	25 minutes	4 (1 salmon fillet)

Storage Tip: Leftovers can be stored in an airtight container in the refrigerator for up to 2 days. Reheat gently in the microwave or oven to avoid overcooking the salmon.

INGREDIENTS

- 4 salmon fillets (4 oz or 113g each)
- 2 tablespoons (30ml) olive oil, divided
- 1 tablespoon (15ml) lemon juice
- 2 cloves garlic, minced
- 1 teaspoon (2g) dried dill
- 1/4 teaspoon (1.5g) salt
- 1/4 teaspoon (0.5g) black pepper
- 1 medium zucchini, sliced
- 1 red bell pepper, cut into chunks
- 1 yellow bell pepper, cut into chunks
- 1 small red onion, cut into wedges
- 1 cup (100g) cherry tomatoes
- 1 tablespoon (4g) fresh parsley, chopped (for garnish)
- Lemon wedges for serving

INSTRUCTIONS

1. Preheat the oven to 400°F (200°C).
2. In a small bowl, mix 1 tablespoon olive oil with lemon juice, minced garlic, dried dill, salt, and pepper.
3. Place salmon fillets on a lightly oiled baking sheet and brush them with the olive oil mixture.
4. In a large bowl, toss the zucchini, bell peppers, onion, and cherry tomatoes with the remaining 1 tablespoon of olive oil. Spread them another baking sheet or around the salmon if there's room.
5. Place both baking sheets in the preheated oven.
6. Roast the vegetables for about 20-25 minutes, stirring once halfway through.
7. Bake the salmon for 12-15 minutes, or until it flakes easily with a fork and reaches an internal temperature of 145°F (63°C).
8. Remove both from the oven.
9. Divide the roasted vegetables among 4 plates and top each with a salmon fillet.
10. Garnish with fresh parsley and serve with lemon wedges.

SPINACH AND FETA STUFFED PORTOBELLO MUSHROOMS

NUTRITIONAL VALUES (PER SERVING)

Calories: 180 *Carbohydrates:* 10g *Fiber:* 3g *Sugars:* 3g *Protein:* 12g *Fat:* 12g

Storage Tip: These stuffed mushrooms can be stored in an airtight container in the refrigerator for up to 2 days. Reheat in the oven at 350°F (175°C) for about 10 minutes or until heated through.

PREP TIME	COOK TIME	SERVINGS
15 minutes	25 minutes	4 (1 stuffed mushroom)

INGREDIENTS

- 4 large portobello mushrooms
- 2 tablespoons (30ml) olive oil, divided
- 1 small onion, finely chopped
- 2 cloves garlic, minced
- 5 oz (140g) fresh spinach, roughly chopped
- 1/4 cup (60ml) low-sodium vegetable broth
- 2 oz (56g) reduced-fat feta cheese, crumbled
- 2 tablespoons (14g) grated Parmesan cheese
- 1/4 cup (30g) chopped walnuts
- 1 teaspoon (2g) dried oregano
- 1/4 teaspoon (1.5g) salt
- 1/4 teaspoon (0.5g) black pepper
- 2 tablespoons (8g) fresh parsley, chopped

INSTRUCTIONS

1. Preheat the oven to 375°F (190°C).
2. Clean the mushrooms and remove the stems. Chop the stems fine and set aside.
3. Brush the mushroom caps with 1 tablespoon of olive oil and place them gill-side up on a baking sheet.
4. In a large skillet, heat the remaining 1 tablespoon of olive oil over medium heat. Add the onion and chopped mushroom stems. Cook for 3-4 minutes until softened.
5. Add minced garlic and cook for another 30 seconds until fragrant.
6. Add chopped spinach and vegetable broth. Cook, stirring occasionally, until the spinach wilts and most of the liquid evaporates, about 3-4 minutes.
7. Remove from heat and stir in crumbled feta, Parmesan cheese, chopped walnuts, oregano, salt, and pepper.
8. Divide the spinach and feta mixture evenly among the mushroom caps.
9. Bake for 20-25 minutes, until the mushrooms are tender and the fill is hot and slightly golden on top.
10. Sprinkle with fresh parsley before serving.

VEGETABLE AND TOFU STIR-FRY WITH BROWN RICE

NUTRITIONAL VALUES (PER SERVING)

Calories: 320 *Carbohydrates:* 40g *Fiber:* 7g *Sugars:* 6g *Protein:* 16g *Fat:* 12g

PREP TIME
20 minutes

COOK TIME
25 minutes

SERVINGS
4

Storage Tip: Store the stir-fry and rice separately in air-tight containers in the refrigerator for up to 3 days. Reheat in the microwave or in a skillet over medium heat.

INGREDIENTS

- 1 cup (185g) brown rice, uncooked
- 14 oz (400g) extra-firm tofu, drained and cubed
- 2 tablespoons (30ml) low-sodium soy sauce, divided
- 2 tablespoons (30ml) sesame oil, divided
- 1 tablespoon (15ml) rice vinegar
- 1 tablespoon (15ml) grated fresh ginger
- 2 cloves garlic, minced
- 1 medium onion, sliced
- 1 red bell pepper, sliced
- 2 cups (140g) broccoli florets
- 1 cup (100g) sliced carrots
- 1 cup (100g) snow peas
- 1/4 cup (60ml) low-sodium vegetable broth
- 1 tablespoon (8g) cornstarch
- 2 green onions, chopped
- 1 tablespoon (9g) sesame seeds

INSTRUCTIONS

1. Cook brown rice according to package instructions. This usually takes about 45 minutes, so start this first.
2. While rice is cooking, press tofu with paper towels to remove excess moisture. Cut into 1-inch cubes.
3. In a small bowl, whisk together 1 tablespoon soy sauce, 1 tablespoon sesame oil, and rice vinegar. Toss tofu cubes in this mixture and let marinate for 10 minutes.
4. Heat a large wok or skillet over medium-high heat. Add the remaining 1 tablespoon sesame oil.
5. Add marinated tofu to the wok and stir-fry until golden brown, about 5-7 minutes. Remove tofu and set aside.
6. In the same wok, add the ginger and garlic. Stir-fry for 30 seconds until fragrant.
7. Add onion, bell pepper, broccoli, and carrots. Stir-fry for 3-4 minutes.
8. Add snow peas and stir-fry for another 2 minutes.
9. In a small bowl, mix vegetable broth, remaining 1 tablespoon soy sauce, and cornstarch.
10. Add the tofu back to the wok with the vegetables. Pour the broth mixture over everything and stir-fry for 2-3 minutes until sauce thickens.
11. Remove from heat and stir in chopped green onions.
12. Serve the stir-fry over brown rice, garnished with sesame seeds.

MEDITERRANEAN CHICKPEA SALAD

NUTRITIONAL VALUES (PER SERVING)

Calories: 280 *Carbohydrates:* 35g *Fiber:* 10g *Sugars:* 6g *Protein:* 12g *Fat:* 12g

Storage Tip: This salad can be stored in an airtight container in the refrigerator for up to 3 days. The flavors often improve after a day, making it a great make-ahead option.

PREP TIME
20 minutes

COOK TIME
0 minutes

SERVINGS
4
(1 1/2 cups)

INGREDIENTS

- 2 cans (15 oz/425g each) chickpeas, drained and rinsed
- 1 English cucumber, diced
- 1 pint (300g) cherry tomatoes, halved
- 1/4 red onion, finely chopped
- 1/2 cup (75g) kalamata olives, pitted and halved
- 1/2 cup (75g) reduced-fat feta cheese, crumbled (optional)
- 1 red bell pepper, diced (optional)
- 1/4 cup (15g) fresh parsley, chopped
- 2 tablespoons (8g) fresh mint, chopped

the dressing:
- 3 tablespoons (45ml) extra-virgin olive oil
- 2 tablespoons (30ml) lemon juice
- 1 clove garlic, minced
- 1 teaspoon (2g) dried oregano
- 1/4 teaspoon (1.5g) salt
- 1/4 teaspoon (0.5g) black pepper

INSTRUCTIONS

1. In a large bowl, combine chickpeas, cucumber, cherry tomatoes, bell pepper, red onion, olives, feta cheese, parsley, and mint.
2. In a small bowl, whisk together olive oil, lemon juice, minced garlic, oregano, salt, and pepper to make the dressing.
3. Pour the dressing over the salad and toss gently to combine all ingredients.
4. Cover and refrigerate for at least 30 minutes to allow flavors to meld.
5. Before serving, give the salad a quick stir and adjust the seasoning if needed.

TUNA AND WHITE BEAN SALAD ON MIXED GREENS

NUTRITIONAL VALUES (PER SERVING)
Calories: 290 Carbohydrates: 25g Fiber: 8g Sugars: 3g Protein: 28g Fat: 10g

PREP TIME 15 minutes | COOK TIME 0 minutes | SERVINGS 4

Storage Tip: The tuna and bean mixture can be stored in an airtight container in the refrigerator for up to 2 days. Keep the mixed greens separate and combine just before serving to maintain freshness.

INGREDIENTS
- 2 cans (5 oz/142g each) chunk light tuna in water, drained
- 1 can (15 oz/425g) white beans (cannellini or Great Northern), drained and rinsed
- 1 cup (150g) cherry tomatoes, halved
- 1/2 red onion, finely chopped
- 1 celery stalk, finely chopped
- 1/4 cup (15g) fresh parsley, chopped
- 2 tablespoons (30ml) extra-virgin olive oil
- 2 tablespoons (30ml) lemon juice
- 1 teaspoon (2g) Dijon mustard
- 1 clove garlic, minced
- 1/4 teaspoon (1.5g) salt
- 1/4 teaspoon (0.5g) black pepper
- 4 cups (120g) mixed salad greens

INSTRUCTIONS
1. In a large bowl, gently combine the drained tuna, white beans, cherry tomatoes, red onion, celery, and parsley.
2. In a small bowl, whisk together olive oil, lemon juice, Dijon mustard, minced garlic, salt, and pepper to make the dressing.
3. Pour the dressing over the tuna and bean mixture. Toss gently to combine all ingredients.
4. Divide the mixed salad greens among 4 plates or bowls (1 cup per serving).
5. Top each bed of greens with approximately 1 1/2 cups of the tuna and bean mixture.
6. Serve immediately.

ZUCCHINI NOODLES WITH LEAN TURKEY MEATBALLS

NUTRITIONAL VALUES (PER SERVING)
Calories: 270 Carbohydrates: 12g Fiber: 4g Sugars: 6g Protein: 28g Fat: 14g

Storage Tip: Store the meatballs and sauce separately from the zucchini noodles in airtight containers in the refrigerator for up to 3 days. Reheat the meatballs and sauce in a skillet, and briefly sauté the zucchini noodles just before serving.

PREP TIME 20 minutes | COOK TIME 25 minutes | SERVINGS 4

INGREDIENTS
For the meatballs:
- 1 lb (450g) lean ground turkey (93% lean)
- 1/4 cup (30g) almond flour
- 1 large egg
- 2 cloves garlic, minced
- 1 teaspoon (2g) dried oregano
- 1/2 teaspoon (3g) salt
- 1/4 teaspoon (0.5g) black pepper

- 1 teaspoon (2g) dried basil
- 1/2 teaspoon (1g) dried oregano
- 1/4 teaspoon (1.5g) salt
- 1/4 teaspoon (0.5g) black pepper
- 2 tablespoons (8g) fresh parsley, chopped
- 2 tablespoons (14g) grated Parmesan cheese (optional)

For the zucchini noodles and sauce:
- 4 medium zucchini
- 2 tablespoons (30ml) olive oil, divided
- 1 small onion, finely chopped
- 2 cloves garlic, minced
- 1 can (14.5 oz/411g) diced tomatoes, no salt added

INSTRUCTIONS
1. In a large bowl, combine ground turkey, almond flour, egg, minced garlic, oregano, salt, and pepper. Mix well and form into 16 small meatballs.
2. Heat 1 tablespoon olive oil in a large skillet over medium heat. Add meatballs and cook, turning occasionally, until browned on all sides and cooked through about 10-12 minutes. Remove meatballs and set aside.
3. In the same skillet, add remaining olive oil and sauté onion until translucent, about 3-4 minutes. Add garlic and cook for another 30 seconds.
4. Add diced tomatoes, basil, oregano, salt, and pepper. Simmer for 10 minutes, stirring occasionally.
5. While the sauce simmers, use a spiralizer or vegetable peeler to create zucchini noodles.
6. Add the meatballs back to the skillet with the sauce and simmer for an additional 5 minutes.
7. In a separate large pan, lightly sauté the zucchini noodles over medium heat for 2-3 minutes, just until slightly softened but still crisp.
8. Divide the zucchini noodles among 4 plates. Top with meatballs and sauce.

DINNER

These recipes are delicious and easy to prepare. It includes a variety of dishes, from hearty stews and casseroles to lighter options like grilled fish and vegetables. Each recipe is designed to be nutritious and satisfying.

BAKED COD WITH VEGETABLES, LEMON, AND HERBS

NUTRITIONAL VALUES (PER SERVING)
Calories: 220 *Carbohydrates:* 10g *Fiber:* 3g *Sugars:* 4g *Protein:* 29g *Fat:* 8g

PREP TIME
15 minutes

COOK TIME
20-25 minutes

SERVINGS
4
(1 cod fillet)

Storage Tip: Store leftovers in an airtight container in the refrigerator for up to 2 days. When reheating, do so gently in the microwave or oven to prevent the fish from becoming tough. For best results, consume within 24 hours of cooking, as seafood tends to be best when fresh.

INGREDIENTS

- 4 cod fillets (about 5 oz/140g each, raw)
- 2 tablespoons (30ml) olive oil
- 2 tablespoons (30ml) fresh lemon juice
- 2 cloves garlic, minced
- 1 teaspoon (1g) dried thyme
- 1 teaspoon (1g) dried oregano
- 1/4 cup (15g) fresh parsley, chopped
- 1/4 teaspoon (1.5g) salt
- 1/4 teaspoon (0.5g) black pepper
- 1 lemon, sliced into rounds
- 1/2 red onion, diced
- 1/2 green pepper, diced
- 1/2 red pepper, diced
- 1/2 yellow pepper, diced
- 2 medium carrots, diced
- *Optional:* lemon wedges for serving

INSTRUCTIONS

1. Preheat the oven to 400°F (200°C).
2. In a small bowl, whisk together olive oil, lemon juice, minced garlic, thyme, oregano, half of the chopped parsley, salt, and pepper.
3. In a large baking dish, combine the diced red onion, green pepper, red pepper, yellow pepper, and carrots. Drizzle with 1 tablespoon of the herb and lemon mixture, toss to coat.
4. Spread the vegetables evenly in the baking dish and place the cod fillets on top.
5. Pour the remaining herb and lemon mixture over the cod, making su to coat each fillet evenly.
6. Top each fillet with a slice of lemon.
7. Bake in the preheated oven for 20-25 minutes, or until the fish flakes easily with a fork and reaches an internal temperature of 145°F (63°C and the vegetables are tender.
8. Remove from the oven and let rest for 5 minutes.
9. Sprinkle the remaining fresh parsley over the cod and vegetables before serving.
10. Serve with additional lemon wedges if desired.

SLOW-COOKER CHICKEN AND VEGETABLE CURRY

NUTRITIONAL VALUES (PER SERVING)
Calories: 290 *Carbohydrates:* 18g *Fiber:* 5g *Sugars:* 6g *Protein:* 28g *Fat:* 12g

Storage Tip: This curry can be stored in an airtight container in the refrigerator for up to 3 days, or frozen for up to 3 months. Reheat gently on the stovetop or in the microwave.

PREP TIME
20 minutes

COOK TIME
6-8h on low or 3-4h on high

SERVINGS
6
(1 1/2 cups)

INGREDIENTS

- 1.5 lbs (680g) boneless, skinless chicken breasts, cut into 1-inch cubes
- 1 large onion, diced
- 2 bell peppers (any color), diced
- 2 medium carrots, sliced
- 1 medium zucchini, diced
- 1 can (14 oz/400ml) light coconut milk
- 1 can (14.5 oz/411g) diced tomatoes, no salt added
- 2 tablespoons (30g) tomato paste
- 2 cloves garlic, minced
- 1 tablespoon (6g) grated fresh ginger
- 2 tablespoons (14g) curry powder
- 1 teaspoon (2g) ground cumin
- 1/2 teaspoon (1g) ground turmeric
- 1/4 teaspoon (0.5g) red pepper flakes (optional)
- 1/2 teaspoon (3g) salt
- 1/4 teaspoon (0.5g) black pepper
- 1 cup (150g) frozen peas
- 1/4 cup (4g) fresh cilantro, chopped
- 1 tablespoon (15ml) lime juice

INSTRUCTIONS

1. In a large slow cooker, combine chicken, onion, bell peppers, carrots and zucchini.
2. In a medium bowl, whisk together coconut milk, diced tomatoes, tomato paste, garlic, ginger, curry powder, cumin, turmeric, red pepper flakes (if using), salt, and black pepper.
3. Pour the sauce mixture over the chicken and vegetables in the slow cooker. Stir to combine.
4. Cover and cook on low for 6-8 hours, or on high for 3-4 hours, until chicken is cooked through and vegetables are tender.
5. 30 minutes before serving, stir in the frozen peas.
6. Just before serving, stir in the fresh cilantro and lime juice.
7. Taste and adjust seasoning if needed.
8. Serve hot.
9. Variation: Swap chicken for firm tofu for a vegetarian version (add t in the last hour of cooking)

GRILLED LEAN STEAK WITH ROASTED ASPARAGUS AND TOMATOES

NUTRITIONAL VALUES (PER SERVING)

Calories: 310 *Carbohydrates:* 10g *Fiber:* 3g *Sugars:* 4g *Protein:* 34g *Fat:* 16g

PREP TIME
15 minutes

COOK TIME
20 minutes

SERVINGS
4
(4 cooked steak)

Storage Tip: Store leftover steak and vegetables separately in airtight containers in the refrigerator for up to 3 days. Reheat the steak gently to avoid overcooking, and reheat the vegetables in the oven to maintain their texture..

INGREDIENTS

For the steak:

- 1 lb (450g) lean sirloin steak, trimmed of visible fat
- 1 tablespoon (15ml) olive oil
- 1 teaspoon (2g) garlic powder
- 1 teaspoon (2g) dried rosemary
- 1/2 teaspoon (3g) salt
- 1/4 teaspoon (0.5g) black pepper

For the vegetables:

- 1 lb (450g) asparagus, tough ends trimmed
- 1 pint (300g) cherry tomatoes
- 2 tablespoons (30ml) olive oil
- 2 cloves garlic, minced
- 1/2 teaspoon (3g) salt
- 1/4 teaspoon (0.5g) black pepper
- 1 tablespoon (15ml) balsamic vinegar

- 2 tablespoons (14g) grated Parmesan cheese (optional)

INSTRUCTIONS

1. Preheat the oven to 400°F (200°C) for the vegetables.
2. In a large bowl, toss asparagus and cherry tomatoes with 2 tablespoons olive oil, minced garlic, salt, and pepper. Spread them on a baking sheet in a single layer.
3. Roast the vegetables for 15-20 minutes, stirring halfway through, until the asparagus is tender and the tomatoes are blistered.
4. While the vegetables are roasting, prepare the steak. Rub the steak with 1 tablespoon olive oil, then season with garlic powder, rosemary, salt, and pepper.
5. Preheat a grill or grill pan over medium-high heat.
6. Grill the steak for about 4-5 minutes per side for medium-rare, or to your desired doneness. The internal temperature should reach 145°F (63°C) for medium-rare.
7. Remove the steak from the grill and let it rest for 5 minutes before slicing.
8. Once the vegetables are done, remove from the oven and toss with balsamic vinegar.
9. Slice the steak against the grain.
10. Serve each portion of steak with 1 cup of roasted vegetables. If using, sprinkle Parmesan cheese over the vegetables.

STUFFED BELL PEPPERS WITH GROUND TURKEY AND QUINOA

NUTRITIONAL VALUES (PER SERVING)

Calories: 310 *Carbohydrates:* 25g *Fiber:* 5g *Sugars:* 6g *Protein:* 28g *Fat:* 12g

Storage Tip: These stuffed peppers can be stored in an airtight container in the refrigerator for up to 3 days. Reheat in the microwave or oven until warmed through.

PREP TIME
20 minutes

COOK TIME
40 minutes

SERVINGS
4
(1 stuffed bell pepper)

INGREDIENTS

- 4 large bell peppers (any color), halved lengthwise and seeds removed
- 1/2 cup (85g) uncooked quinoa
- 1 cup (240ml) low-sodium chicken broth
- 1 lb (450g) lean ground turkey (93% lean)
- 1 tablespoon (15ml) olive oil
- 1 small onion, finely chopped
- 2 cloves garlic, minced
- 1 can (14.5 oz/411g) diced tomatoes, no salt added, drained
- 1 teaspoon (2g) dried oregano
- 1 teaspoon (2g) ground cumin
- 1/2 teaspoon (3g) salt
- 1/4 teaspoon (0.5g) black pepper
- 1/4 cup (15g) fresh parsley, chopped
- 1/2 cup (56g) reduced-fat shredded cheddar cheese

INSTRUCTIONS

1. Preheat the oven to 375°F (190°C).
2. In a medium saucepan, combine quinoa and chicken broth. Bring to a boil, then reduce heat to low, cover, and simmer for about 15 minutes or until quinoa is tender and liquid is absorbed.
3. While quinoa is cooking, heat olive oil in a large skillet over medium heat. Add onion and cook until softened, about 5 minutes.
4. Add garlic and cook for another 30 seconds until fragrant.
5. Add ground turkey to the skillet and cook, breaking it up with a spatula, until no longer pink, about 7-8 minutes.
6. Stir in drained diced tomatoes, oregano, cumin, salt, and pepper. Cook for another 2-3 minutes.
7. Remove from heat and stir in the cooked quinoa and chopped parsley.
8. Arrange the bell pepper halves in a large baking dish. Fill each pepper half with the turkey-quinoa mixture.
9. Cover the baking dish with foil and bake for 30 minutes.
10. Remove foil, sprinkle cheese over the peppers, and bake uncovered for an additional 5-10 minutes, until cheese is melted and peppers are tender.
11. Let cool for 5 minutes before serving.

SHRIMP AND BROCCOLI STIR-FRY

NUTRITIONAL VALUES (PER SERVING)

Calories: 220 *Carbohydrates:* 12g *Fiber:* 4g *Sugars:* 3g *Protein:* 26g *Fat:* 9g

PREP TIME
15
minutes

COOK TIME
10
minutes

SERVINGS
4
(1 1/2 cups)

Storage Tip: This stir-fry can be stored in an airtight container in the refrigerator for up to 2 days. Reheat gently in a skillet or microwave to avoid overcooking the shrimp.

INGREDIENTS

- 1 lb (450g) medium shrimp, peeled and deveined
- 4 cups (280g) broccoli florets
- 2 tablespoons (30ml) avocado oil or canola oil, divided
- 2 cloves garlic, minced
- 1 tablespoon (6g) grated fresh ginger
- 1/4 cup (60ml) low-sodium chicken broth
- 2 tablespoons (30ml) low-sodium soy sauce
- 1 tablespoon (15ml) rice vinegar
- 1 teaspoon (5g) cornstarch
- 1/4 teaspoon (0.5g) red pepper flakes (optional)
- 2 green onions, sliced
- 1 tablespoon (9g) sesame seeds

INSTRUCTIONS

1. In a small bowl, whisk together chicken broth, soy sauce, rice vinegar, and cornstarch. Set aside.
2. Heat 1 tablespoon of oil in a large wok or skillet over medium-high heat.
3. Add shrimp to the wok and cook for about 2-3 minutes, stirring occasionally, until they turn pink. Remove shrimp from the wok and set aside.
4. In the same wok, add the remaining 1 tablespoon of oil. Add broccoli florets and stir-fry for 3-4 minutes until they're bright green and slightly tender.
5. Add minced garlic and grated ginger to the wok. Stir-fry for about 30 seconds until fragrant.
6. Pour the sauce mixture into the wok. Cook, stirring constantly, until the sauce thickens slightly, about 1-2 minutes.
7. Return the cooked shrimp to the wok and add red pepper flakes if using. Stir to combine everything and cook for an additional 1-2 minutes until shrimp is heated through and broccoli is tender-crisp.
8. Remove from heat and stir in sliced green onions.
9. Sprinkle with sesame seeds before serving.

VEGETARIAN CHILI WITH MIXED BEANS

NUTRITIONAL VALUES (PER SERVING)

Calories: 280 *Carbohydrates:* 45g *Fiber:* 14g *Sugars:* 8g *Protein:* 15g *Fat:* 6g

Storage Tip: This chili can be stored in an airtight container in the refrigerator for up to 4 days or frozen for up to 3 months. Reheat gently on the stovetop or in the microwave.

PREP TIME
15
minutes

COOK TIME
40 minutes

SERVINGS
6
(1 1/2 cups)

INGREDIENTS

- 1 tablespoon (15ml) olive oil
- 1 large onion, diced
- 2 bell peppers (any color), diced
- 3 cloves garlic, minced
- 2 carrots, diced
- 2 celery stalks, diced
- 1 can (14.5 oz/411g) diced tomatoes, no salt added
- 1 can (6 oz/170g) tomato paste
- 3 cups (720ml) low-sodium vegetable broth
- 1 can (15 oz/425g) black beans, drained and rinsed
- 1 can (15 oz/425g) kidney beans, drained and rinsed
- 1 can (15 oz/425g) pinto beans, drained and rinsed
- 1 cup (170g) frozen corn kernels
- 2 tablespoons (14g) chili powder

- 1 tablespoon (6g) ground cumin
- 1 teaspoon (2g) dried oregano
- 1/2 teaspoon (1g) smoked paprika
- 1/4 teaspoon (0.5g) cayenne pepper (optional)
- 1/2 teaspoon (3g) salt
- 1/4 teaspoon (0.5g) black pepper
- 1/4 cup (4g) fresh cilantro, chopped

Optional toppings:
- diced avocado
- plain Greek yogurt
- sliced jalapeños

INSTRUCTIONS

1. Heat olive oil in a large pot over medium heat. Add onion, bell peppers, garlic, carrots, and celery. Cook for 5-7 minutes until vegetables start to soften.
2. Add diced tomatoes, tomato paste, and vegetable broth to the pot. Stir to combine.
3. Add black beans, kidney beans, pinto beans, and corn to the pot. Stir well.
4. Add chili powder, cumin, oregano, smoked paprika, cayenne pepper (if using), salt, and black pepper. Stir to combine all ingredients.
5. Bring the chili to a boil, then reduce the heat to low. Simmer, uncovered, for 30 minutes, stirring occasionally.
6. Taste and adjust seasoning if needed.
7. Stir in chopped cilantro just before serving.
8. Serve hot, with optional toppings if desired.

BAKED EGGPLANT PARMESAN

NUTRITIONAL VALUES (PER SERVING)

Calories: 250 *Carbohydrates:* 25g *Fiber:* 8g *Sugars:* 9g *Protein:* 15g *Fat:* 12g

PREP TIME	COOK TIME	SERVINGS
25 minutes	45 minutes	6 (1/6 of the dish)

Storage Tip: Store leftovers in an airtight container in the refrigerator for up to 3 days. Reheat in the oven at 350ºF (175ºC) for about 10 minutes to maintain crispiness.

INGREDIENTS

2 large eggplants (about 2 lbs/900g total), sliced into 1/4-inch rounds
1 cup (120g) whole-grain breadcrumbs
1/4 cup (25g) grated Parmesan cheese
1 teaspoon (2g) dried oregano
1 teaspoon (2g) dried basil
1/4 teaspoon (0.5g) garlic powder
1/4 teaspoon (1.5g) salt
1/4 teaspoon (0.5g) black pepper
2 large eggs, beaten
2 cups (480ml) low-sodium marinara sauce
1 cup (112g) part-skim mozzarella cheese, shredded
2 tablespoons (8g) fresh basil, chopped (for garnish)
Olive oil cooking spray

INSTRUCTIONS

1. Preheat the oven to 400ºF (200ºC). Line two baking sheets with parchment paper.
2. In a shallow bowl, mix together whole-grain breadcrumbs, Parmesan cheese, dried oregano, dried basil, garlic powder, salt, and pepper.
3. Dip each eggplant slice in beaten egg, then coat with the breadcrumb mixture. Place on the prepared baking sheets.
4. Lightly spray the breaded eggplant slices with olive oil cooking spray.
5. Bake for 20 minutes, then flip the slices and bake for another 10 minutes, until golden brown and crispy.
6. Reduce oven temperature to 350ºF (175ºC).
7. In a 9x13-inch baking dish, spread 1/2 cup of marinara sauce.
8. Layer half of the baked eggplant slices over the sauce.
9. Spread another 1/2 cup of marinara sauce over the eggplant, then sprinkle with 1/2 cup of mozzarella cheese.
10. Repeat with another layer of eggplant, sauce, and cheese.
11. Bake for 15-20 minutes, until the cheese is melted and bubbly.
12. Let cool for 5 minutes before serving. Garnish with fresh basil.

GRILLED PORK TENDERLOIN WITH ROASTED SWEET POTATOES

NUTRITIONAL VALUES (PER SERVING)

Calories: 320 *Carbohydrates:* 23g *Fiber:* 3g *Sugars:* 7g *Protein:* 32g *Fat:* 10g

Storage Tip: Store leftover pork and sweet potatoes separately in airtight containers in the refrigerator for up to 3 days. Reheat pork gently to avoid overcooking, and reheat sweet potatoes in the oven to maintain their texture.

PREP TIME	COOK TIME	SERVINGS
20 minutes	40 minutes	4 (1 cooked pork)

INGREDIENTS

For the pork tenderloin:

1 lb (450g) pork tenderloin
2 tablespoons (30ml) olive oil
3 cloves garlic, minced
1 tablespoon (6g) fresh rosemary, chopped
1 teaspoon (2g) dried thyme
1 teaspoon (6g) Dijon mustard
1/2 teaspoon (3g) salt
1/4 teaspoon (0.5g) black pepper

For the sweet potatoes:

2 medium sweet potatoes (about 1 lb/450g total), peeled and cubed
1 tablespoon (15ml) olive oil
1/2 teaspoon (1g) ground cinnamon
1/4 teaspoon (1.5g) salt
1/4 teaspoon (0.5g) black pepper

INSTRUCTIONS

1. Preheat the oven to 400ºF (200ºC) for the sweet potatoes.
2. In a small bowl, mix olive oil, minced garlic, rosemary, thyme, Dijon mustard, salt, and pepper to create a marinade for the pork.
3. Rub the marinade all over the pork tenderloin. Let it marinate at room temperature for 15 minutes while you prepare the sweet potatoes.
4. In a large bowl, toss sweet potato cubes with olive oil, cinnamon, salt, and pepper.
5. Spread the sweet potatoes on a baking sheet in a single layer. Roast in the preheated oven for 25-30 minutes, stirring halfway through, until tender and lightly caramelized.
6. While the sweet potatoes are roasting, preheat the grill or grill pan to medium-high heat.
7. Grill the pork tenderloin for about 15-18 minutes, turning every 4-5 minutes, until it reaches an internal temperature of 145ºF (63ºC).
8. Remove the pork from the grill and let it rest for 5 minutes before slicing.
9. Slice the pork tenderloin into 1/2-inch thick rounds.
10. Serve 4 oz of sliced pork tenderloin with 1/2 cup of roasted sweet potatoes per person.

CAULIFLOWER RICE BURRITO BOWL

NUTRITIONAL VALUES (PER SERVING)
Calories: 310 *Carbohydrates:* 20g *Fiber:* 8g *Sugars:* 5g *Protein:* 28g *Fat:* 15g

PREP TIME
20
minutes

COOK TIME
20
minutes

SERVINGS
4
(1 bowl)

Storage Tip: Store the components separately in airtight containers in the refrigerator for up to 3 days. Assemble just before eating to keep the vegetables fresh and crisp.

INGREDIENTS

For the cauliflower rice:
- 1 medium head cauliflower, riced (about 4 cups)
- 1 tablespoon (15ml) olive oil
- 2 cloves garlic, minced
- 1/4 cup (4g) fresh cilantro, chopped
- 1 lime, juiced
- 1/4 teaspoon (1.5g) salt

For the chicken:
- 1 lb (450g) boneless, skinless chicken breast, cut into bite-sized pieces
- 1 tablespoon (15ml) olive oil
- 2 teaspoons (4g) chili powder
- 1 teaspoon (2g) ground cumin
- 1/2 teaspoon (1g) paprika
- 1/4 teaspoon (1.5g) salt

- 1/4 teaspoon (0.5g) black pepper

For the bowl:
- 1 can (15 oz/425g) black beans, drained and rinsed
- 1 cup (150g) tomatoes, halved
- 1 bell pepper, any color, diced
- 1 small red onion, finely diced
- 1 avocado, sliced
- 4 tablespoons (60g) plain Greek yogurt (optional)
- Hot sauce to taste (optional)

INSTRUCTIONS

1. To make cauliflower rice: Heat 1 tablespoon olive oil in a large skillet over medium heat. Add minced garlic and sauté for 30 seconds. Add riced cauliflower and cook for 5-7 minutes, stirring occasionally, until tender. Remove from heat, stir in cilantro, lime juice, and salt. Set aside
2. For the chicken: In a bowl, mix chili powder, cumin, paprika, salt, and pepper. Toss chicken pieces with this spice mixture.
3. Heat 1 tablespoon olive oil in a large skillet over medium-high heat. Add seasoned chicken and cook for 6-8 minutes, stirring occasiona until fully cooked and slightly browned.
4. To assemble the bowls: Divide the cauliflower rice among 4 bowls. T each with equal portions of cooked chicken, black beans, cherry tomatoes, bell pepper, and red onion.
5. Add sliced avocado to each bowl.
6. Top each bowl with 1 tablespoon of Greek yogurt (optional)
7. Add hot sauce if desired.

Variations
Leave out the chicken and replace with chickpeas for a meat-free dish.

CHICKPEA AND SPINACH CURRY

NUTRITIONAL VALUES (PER SERVING)

Calories: 300 *Carbohydrates:* 40g *Fiber:* 11g *Sugars:* 8g *Protein:* 13g *Fat:* 12g

Storage Tip: Store in an airtight container in the refrigerator for up to 3-4 days. The flavors often improve after a day, making this a great make-ahead meal. Reheat gently on the stovetop or in the microwave, adding a splash of water if needed to loosen the sauce..

PREP TIME
15
minutes

COOK TIME
30 minutes

SERVINGS
4
(1.5 cups)

INGREDIENTS
- 2 tablespoons (30ml) coconut oil
- 1 large onion, finely chopped
- 1 carrot, diced
- 3 cloves garlic, minced
- 1 tablespoon (15g) grated fresh ginger
- 2 teaspoons (4g) ground cumin
- 2 teaspoons (4g) ground coriander
- 1 teaspoon (2g) turmeric
- 1/4 teaspoon (0.5g) cayenne pepper (adjust to taste)
- 2 cans (15 oz/425g each) chickpeas, drained and rinsed
- 1 can (14 oz/400g) diced tomatoes
- 1 can (14 oz/400ml) light coconut milk
- 4 cups (120g) fresh spinach, roughly chopped
- Salt to taste
- 1/4 cup (4g) fresh cilantro, chopped
- Juice of 1 lime
- *Optional:* Brown rice or naan bread for serving

INSTRUCTIONS
1. Heat coconut oil in a large pot over medium heat. Add the choppe onion and cook for 5-7 minutes until softened and translucent.
2. Add minced garlic and grated ginger. Cook for another 1-2 minutes until fragrant.
3. Stir in the ground cumin, coriander, turmeric, and cayenne pepper. Toast the spices for about 30 seconds until fragrant.
4. Add the drained chickpeas, diced tomatoes (with their juice), and coconut milk. Stir to combine.
5. Bring the mixture to a simmer, then reduce heat to low and cook fo 15-20 minutes, stirring occasionally, until the sauce has thickened slightly.
6. Add the chopped spinach and stir until it wilts, about 2-3 minutes.
7. Season with salt to taste.
8. Remove from heat and stir in the fresh cilantro and lime juice.
9. Serve hot, optionally over brown rice or with naan bread.

SNACK

This section offers a selection of healthy sweet and savory snacks that are perfect for satisfying cravings between meals without compromising on nutrition.

CHIA SEED PUDDING SNACK CUPS

NUTRITIONAL VALUES (PER SERVING)

Calories: 180 *Carbohydrates:* 15g *Fiber:* 10g *Sugars:* 3g *Protein:* 7g *Fat:* 12g

PREP TIME	COOK TIME	SERVINGS
15 minutes	10 minutes	4 (1 pudding cup)

Storage Tip: The prepared chia seed pudding (without toppings) can be stored in an airtight container in the refrigerator for up to 5 days. Add fresh toppings just before serving..

INGREDIENTS

For the base: .
- 1/4 cup (40g) chia seeds
- 1 cup (240ml) unsweetened almond milk
- 1 teaspoon (5ml) vanilla extract
- 1/4 teaspoon ground cinnamon
- 1 tablespoon (15ml) sugar-free maple syrup (optional)

For the toppings (per serving):
- 1/4 cup (40g) mixed berries (strawberries, blueberries, raspberries)
- 1 tablespoon (7g) sliced almonds
- 1/2 tablespoon (7g) unsweetened shredded coconut

INSTRUCTIONS

1. In a medium bowl, whisk together chia seeds, almond milk, vanilla extract, cinnamon, and sugar-free maple syrup (if using) until well combined.
2. Cover the bowl with plastic wrap or transfer the mixture to an airtight container.
3. Refrigerate for at least 4 hours or overnight, until the mixture has thickened to a pudding-like consistency.
4. Once chilled, stir the pudding well to break up any clumps.
5. Divide the chia seed pudding evenly among 4 small cups or jars.
6. Top each pudding cup with 1/4 cup of mixed berries, 1 tablespoon of sliced almonds, and 1/2 tablespoon of unsweetened shredded coconut.
7. Serve chilled.

LOW-GI SEED AND NUT BARS

NUTRITIONAL VALUES (PER SERVING)

Calories: 190 *Carbohydrates:* 12g *Fiber:* 4g *Sugars:* 3g *Protein:* 7g *Fat:* 14g

Storage Tip: Store the bars in an airtight container at room temperature for up to 5 days, or in the refrigerator for up to 2 weeks. You can also freeze them for up to 3 months..

PREP TIME	COOK TIME	SERVINGS
15 minutes	25 m. (+ 1 h. Cool Time)	12 (1 bar)

INGREDIENTS

- 1 cup (150g) mixed nuts (almonds, walnuts, pecans)
- 1/2 cup (70g) pumpkin seeds
- 1/4 cup (35g) sunflower seeds
- 1/4 cup (40g) chia seeds
- 1/4 cup (20g) unsweetened shredded coconut
- 2 tablespoons (14g) ground flaxseed
- 1/4 cup (60ml) sugar-free maple syrup
- 2 tablespoons (32g) almond butter
- 1 large egg white
- 1 teaspoon (5ml) vanilla extract
- 1/4 teaspoon salt
- 1/4 teaspoon ground cinnamon

INSTRUCTIONS

1. Preheat the oven to 325°F (165°C). Line an 8x8 inch baking pan with parchment paper, leaving some overhang for easy removal.
2. In a large bowl, combine mixed nuts, pumpkin seeds, sunflower seed chia seeds, shredded coconut, and ground flaxseed.
3. In a separate small bowl, whisk together sugar-free maple syrup, almond butter, egg white, vanilla extract, salt, and cinnamon until well combined.
4. Pour the wet ingredients over the dry ingredients and mix thoroughl until everything is well coated.
5. Transfer the mixture to the prepared baking pan. Press down firmly and evenly using the back of a spoon or your hands.
6. Bake for 23-25 minutes, or until the edges are golden brown.
7. Remove from the oven and let cool in the pan for 10 minutes.
8. Using the parchment paper overhang, lift the bars out of the pan ar place on a wire rack to cool completely (about 1 hour).
9. Once cooled, cut into 12 bars.

BAKED ZUCCHINI CHIPS

NUTRITIONAL VALUES (PER SERVING)

Calories: 45 *Carbohydrates:* 5g *Fiber:* 2g *Sugars:* 3g *Protein:* 2g *Fat:* 2g

PREP TIME
15 minutes

COOK TIME
2 hours

SERVINGS
4
(1 cup of chips)

Storage Tip: Store in an airtight container at room temperature for up to 3 days. If they lose their crispness, you can re-crisp them in the oven at 200°F (95°C) for about 10 minutes.

INGREDIENTS

- medium zucchini (about 1 pound or 450g total)
- tablespoon (15ml) olive oil
- 4 teaspoon salt
- 4 teaspoon black pepper
- 4 teaspoon garlic powder
- 4 teaspoon paprika

INSTRUCTIONS

1. Preheat the oven to 225°F (110°C). Line two large baking sheets with parchment paper.
2. Wash and dry the zucchini. Using a mandoline or a sharp knife, slice the zucchini into very thin rounds, about 1/8 inch thick.
3. Place the zucchini slices in a large bowl. Drizzle with olive oil and toss gently to coat all slices evenly.
4. In a small bowl, mix together salt, black pepper, garlic powder, and paprika.
5. Sprinkle the seasoning mixture over the zucchini slices and toss gently to distribute evenly.
6. Arrange the zucchini slices in a single layer on the prepared baking sheets. Make sure the slices don't overlap.
7. Bake for about 2 hours, rotating the baking sheets halfway through. The chips are done when they're crispy and golden brown.
8. Remove from the oven and let cool on the baking sheets for about 5 minutes. They will crisp up more as they cool.
9. Once cooled, transfer to a serving bowl.

HOMEMADE HUMMUS WITH VEGETABLE CRUDITÉS

NUTRITIONAL VALUES (PER SERVING)

Calories: 150 *Carbohydrates:* 15g *Fiber:* 6g *Sugars:* 4g *Protein:* 6g *Fat:* 8g

Storage Tip: Store hummus in an airtight container in the refrigerator for up to 5 days. Prepare vegetable crudités fresh for best quality, or store cut vegetables in water in the refrigerator for up to 2 days..

PREP TIME
20 minutes

COOK TIME
0 minutes

SERVINGS
6
(1/4 cup hummus)

INGREDIENTS

The hummus:
- can (15 oz/425g) chickpeas, drained and rinsed
- tablespoons (30ml) lemon juice
- tablespoons (30ml) olive oil
- tablespoons (30ml) water
- love garlic, minced
- teaspoon ground cumin
- teaspoon salt
- teaspoon paprika (for garnish)

The vegetable crudités (6 cups total):
- cups cucumber slices
- up baby carrots
- up bell pepper strips (mixed colors)
- up cherry tomatoes
- up celery sticks

INSTRUCTIONS

1. Drain and rinse the chickpeas. If time allows, remove the skins for a smoother hummus.
2. In a food processor, combine chickpeas, lemon juice, olive oil, water, minced garlic, cumin, and salt.
3. Process until smooth, stopping to scrape down the sides as needed. If the hummus is too thick, add water, one tablespoon at a time, until the desired consistency is reached.
4. Taste and adjust seasonings if needed.
5. Transfer the hummus to a serving bowl and sprinkle with paprika.
6. Wash and prepare the vegetables for the crudités.
7. Arrange the hummus bowl in the center of a large platter and surround it with the prepared vegetables.

ALMOND FLOUR CRACKERS

NUTRITIONAL VALUES (PER SERVING)

Calories: 140 *Carbohydrates:* 5g *Fiber:* 3g *Sugars:* 1g *Protein:* 6g *Fat:* 12g

PREP TIME	COOK TIME	SERVINGS
15 minutes	15-20 minutes	8 (10 crackers)

Storage Tip: Store in an airtight container at room temperature for up to 5 days. For longer storage, keep in the refrigerator for up to 2 weeks.

INGREDIENTS

- 2 cups (224g) almond flour
- 1 large egg
- 2 tablespoons (30ml) olive oil
- 1/2 teaspoon salt
- 1 teaspoon dried rosemary (optional)
- sesame seed (optional)
- 1/4 teaspoon garlic powder (optional)

INSTRUCTIONS

1. Preheat the oven to 350°F (175°C). Line a large baking sheet with parchment paper.
2. In a large bowl, combine almond flour, salt, and if using, rosemary garlic powder.
3. In a small bowl, whisk together the egg and olive oil.
4. Add the wet ingredients to the dry ingredients and mix well to form a dough.
5. Place the dough between two sheets of parchment paper and roll out to about 1/8 inch thickness.
6. Remove the top sheet of parchment paper and transfer the bottom sheet with the rolled dough onto the baking sheet.
7. Using a knife or pizza cutter, score the dough into approximately 8 small crackers.
8. Bake for 15-20 minutes, until the edges are golden brown.
9. Remove from the oven and let cool completely on the baking sheet. The crackers will crisp up as they cool.
10. Once cooled, break the crackers along the scored lines.

GREEK YOGURT BARK WITH BERRIES AND NUTS

NUTRITIONAL VALUES (PER SERVING)

Calories: 110 *Carbohydrates:* 8g *Fiber:* 2g *Sugars:* 4g *Protein:* 8g *Fat:* 6g

Storage Tip: Store the yogurt bark pieces in an airtight container or freezer bag in the freezer for up to 1 month. Let sit at room temperature for 1-2 minutes before eating for the best texture...

PREP TIME	FREEZE TIME	SERVINGS
15 minutes	3 hours	8 (1 piece)

INGREDIENTS

- 2 cups (500g) plain, non-fat Greek yogurt
- 1 teaspoon vanilla extract
- 2 tablespoons (30ml) sugar-free maple syrup or liquid stevia to taste
- 1/2 cup (75g) mixed fresh berries (strawberries, blueberries, raspberries)
- 1/4 cup (30g) chopped mixed nuts (almonds, walnuts, pecans)
- 2 tablespoons (20g) unsweetened shredded coconut
- 1 tablespoon (15g) sugar-free dark chocolate chips (optional)

INSTRUCTIONS

1. Line a baking sheet with parchment paper.
2. In a medium bowl, mix Greek yogurt, vanilla extract, and sugar-free maple syrup or stevia until well combined.
3. Spread the yogurt mixture evenly on the prepared baking sheet to about 1/4 inch thickness.
4. Scatter the mixed berries, chopped nuts, and shredded coconut evenly over the yogurt. If using, sprinkle the dark chocolate chips as well.
5. Gently press the toppings into the yogurt to ensure they stick.
6. Place the baking sheet in the freezer for at least 3 hours or until the yogurt is completely frozen.
7. Once frozen, break or cut the bark into approximately 8 pieces.
8. Serve immediately or store in the freezer.

BAKED SWEET POTATO FRIES

NUTRITIONAL VALUES (PER SERVING)

Calories: 120 *Carbohydrates:* 22g *Fiber:* 4g *Sugars:* 5g *Protein:* 2g *Fat:* 3g

PREP TIME 15 minutes **COOK TIME** 25–30 minutes **SERVINGS** 4 (about 1 cup)

Storage Tip: These fries are best served immediately. If you have leftovers, store them in an airtight container in the refrigerator for up to 3 days. Reheat in the oven at 400ºF (200ºC) for about 5 minutes to regain crispness..

INGREDIENTS

2 medium sweet potatoes (about 400g total), peeled
1 tablespoon (15ml) olive oil
1/2 teaspoon salt
1/4 teaspoon black pepper
1/2 teaspoon paprika
1/4 teaspoon garlic powder
1/8 teaspoon cayenne pepper (optional)

INSTRUCTIONS

1. Preheat the oven to 425ºF (220ºC). Line a large baking sheet with parchment paper.
2. Cut the sweet potatoes into even fries, about 1/4 inch thick. Try to keep them uniform in size for even cooking.
3. In a large bowl, toss the sweet potato fries with olive oil until evenly coated.
4. In a small bowl, mix together salt, black pepper, paprika, garlic powder, and cayenne pepper (if using).
5. Sprinkle the spice mixture over the oiled sweet potato fries and toss to coat evenly.
6. Arrange the fries in a single layer on the prepared baking sheet, ensuring they don't overlap.
7. Bake for 15 minutes, then remove from the oven and flip the fries.
8. Return to the oven and bake for an additional 10-15 minutes, or until the fries are crispy and lightly browned on the edges.
9. Remove from the oven and let cool for a few minutes before serving.

AVOCADO AND BLACK BEAN DIP

NUTRITIONAL VALUES (PER SERVING)

Calories: 110 *Carbohydrates:* 12g *Fiber:* 6g *Sugars:* 1g *Protein:* 4g *Fat:* 6g

Storage Tip: Store in an airtight container in the refrigerator with plastic wrap pressed directly onto the surface of the dip to prevent browning. Best consumed within 2 days.

PREP TIME 15 minutes **COOK TIME** 0 minutes **SERVINGS** 8 (1/4 cup)

INGREDIENTS

1 can (15 oz/425g) black beans, drained and rinsed
2 medium ripe avocados, pitted and peeled
1/4 cup (60ml) fresh lime juice (about 2 limes)
1/4 cup (15g) fresh cilantro, chopped
1/2 small red onion, finely chopped
2 cloves garlic, minced
1 small jalapeño, seeded and finely chopped (optional)
1 teaspoon ground cumin
1/2 teaspoon salt
1/4 teaspoon black pepper

INSTRUCTIONS

1. In a food processor, combine the black beans, avocados, and lime juice. Pulse until the mixture is mostly smooth, with some chunks remaining for texture.
2. Add the cilantro, red onion, garlic, jalapeño (if using), cumin, salt, and black pepper to the food processor. Pulse a few times to incorporate, but don't over-process.
3. Taste and adjust seasoning if needed, adding more salt, pepper, or lime juice as desired.
4. Transfer the dip to a serving bowl.
5. Serve immediately, or for best flavor, cover tightly with plastic wrap (pressing the wrap directly onto the surface of the dip to prevent browning) and refrigerate for at least 30 minutes to allow flavors to meld.

FLAXSEED AND ALMOND MEAL MUFFINS

NUTRITIONAL VALUES (PER SERVING)

Calories: 165 *Carbohydrates:* 8g *Fiber:* 4g *Sugars:* 2g *Protein:* 6g *Fat:* 13g

PREP TIME
15
minutes

COOK TIME
20
minutes

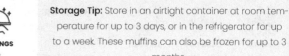

SERVINGS
12
(1 muffin)

Storage Tip: Store in an airtight container at room temperature for up to 3 days, or in the refrigerator for up to a week. These muffins can also be frozen for up to 3 months..

INGREDIENTS

- 1 cup (96g) almond meal
- 1/2 cup (56g) ground flaxseed
- 1/4 cup (28g) coconut flour
- 1 tsp (5g) baking powder
- 1/2 tsp (3g) salt
- 1/4 tsp (1g) ground cinnamon
- 4 large eggs
- 1/4 cup (60ml) unsweetened almond milk
- 1/4 cup (60ml) melted coconut oil
- 2 tbsp (30ml) sugar-free maple syrup
- 1 tsp (5ml) vanilla extract
- 1/2 cup (50g) chopped walnuts

INSTRUCTIONS

1. Preheat the oven to 350ºF (175ºC). Line a 12-cup muffin tin with paper liners or grease with cooking spray.
2. In a large bowl, whisk together almond meal, ground flaxseed, coconut flour, baking powder, salt, and cinnamon.
3. In a separate bowl, beat the eggs. Add almond milk, melted coconut oil, sugar-free maple syrup, and vanilla extract. Mix well.
4. Pour the wet ingredients into the dry ingredients. Stir until just combined.
5. Fold in the chopped walnuts.
6. Divide the batter evenly among the prepared muffin cups, filling each about 2/3 full.
7. Bake for 18-20 minutes, or until a toothpick inserted into the center of muffin comes out clean.
8. Remove from the oven and let cool in the tin for 5 minutes.
9. Transfer muffins to a wire rack to cool completely.

ROASTED CHICKPEA SNACK MIX

NUTRITIONAL VALUES (PER SERVING)

Calories: 180 *Carbohydrates:* 20g *Fiber:* 6g *Sugars:* 2g *Protein:* 8g *Fat:* 8g

Storage Tip: Store in an airtight container at room temperature for up to 1 week. If the mix loses its crispness, you can refresh it in a 350ºF (175ºC) oven for 5-10 minutes.

PREP TIME
15
minutes

COOK TIME
25 m.
(+ 1 h.
Cool Time)

SERVINGS
6
(1/2 cup)

INGREDIENTS

- 2 cans (15 oz each) chickpeas, drained and rinsed
- 2 tbsp (30ml) olive oil
- 1 tsp (5g) smoked paprika
- 1 tsp (5g) garlic powder
- 1 tsp (5g) onion powder
- 1/2 tsp (3g) salt
- 1/4 tsp (1g) black pepper
- 1/2 cup (60g) raw almonds
- 1/2 cup (30g) unsweetened coconut flakes
- 1/4 cup (30g) pumpkin seeds
- ¼ cup (30g) dried blueberries

INSTRUCTIONS

1. Preheat the oven to 400ºF (200ºC).
2. Pat the chickpeas dry with a clean kitchen towel or paper towels. Remove any loose skins.
3. In a large bowl, mix the chickpeas with 1 1/2 tbsp olive oil, smoked paprika, garlic powder, onion powder, salt, and pepper.
4. Spread the seasoned chickpeas on a large baking sheet in a single layer.
5. Roast for 20-25 minutes, shaking the pan halfway through, until the chickpeas are crispy.
6. While the chickpeas are roasting, mix the almonds and pumpkin seeds with the remaining 1/2 tbsp of olive oil in a small bowl.
7. After the chickpeas have roasted for 20-25 minutes, add the almonds and pumpkin seed mixture to the baking sheet.
8. Roast for an additional 5 minutes, then add the coconut flakes and roast for 2-3 more minutes until the coconut is lightly toasted. Watch carefully to prevent burning.
9. Remove from the oven and let cool completely on the baking sheet.
10. Once cooled, mix all components together in a large bowl.

DESSERT

Indulge your sweet tooth with these carefully crafted dessert recipes that offer a perfect balance of flavor and nutrition, allowing you to enjoy treats while managing your blood sugar levels effectively.

SUGAR-FREE CHOCOLATE AVOCADO MOUSSE

NUTRITIONAL VALUES (PER SERVING)
Calories: 220 *Carbohydrates:* 15g *Fiber:* 9g *Sugars:* 2g *Protein:* 4g *Fat:* 18g

PREP TIME
15 minutes

CHILL TIME
2 hours

SERVINGS
4
(1/2 cup)

Storage Tip: This mousse can be stored in the refrigerator, covered, for up to 3 days. The avocado may cause slight discoloration over time, but this doesn't affect the taste.

INGREDIENTS

- 2 ripe medium avocados, pitted and peeled (about 300g)
- 1/4 cup (25g) unsweetened cocoa powder
- 1/4 cup (60ml) unsweetened almond milk
- 3 tbsp (45ml) sugar-free maple syrup
- 2 tsp (10ml) vanilla extract
- 1/8 tsp (0.5g) salt
- 2 oz (56g) sugar-free dark chocolate, melted and cooled
- *Optional:* Sugar-free whipped cream for topping

INSTRUCTIONS

1. In a food processor or high-powered blender, combine the avocado, cocoa powder, almond milk, sugar-free maple syrup, vanilla extract, and salt.
2. Blend until smooth, stopping to scrape down the sides as needed.
3. Add the melted and cooled sugar-free dark chocolate to the mixture.
4. Blend again until the chocolate is fully incorporated and the mousse is smooth and creamy.
5. Taste and adjust sweetness if needed by adding more sugar-free maple syrup, 1 teaspoon at a time.
6. Divide the mousse evenly among 4 small serving dishes or ramekins.
7. Cover with plastic wrap, making sure the wrap touches the surface of the mousse to prevent a skin from forming.
8. Refrigerate for at least 2 hours or until chilled and set.
9. Before serving, let the mousse sit at room temperature for about 5 minutes to soften slightly.
10. If desired, top with a dollop of sugar-free whipped cream before serving.

GREEK YOGURT CHEESECAKE WITH ALMOND CRUST

NUTRITIONAL VALUES (PER SERVING)
Calories: 220 *Carbohydrates:* 10g *Fiber:* 2g *Sugars:* 5g *Protein:* 10g *Fat:* 16g

Storage Tip: Store covered in the refrigerator for up to 5 days. This cheesecake can also be frozen for up to 2 months. Thaw overnight in the refrigerator before serving.

PREP TIME
20 minutes

COOK TIME
50 m
(+4 h chill time)

SERVINGS
12
(1 slice)

INGREDIENTS

For the crust:
- 2 cups (224g) almond flour
- 3 tbsp (45g) melted unsalted butter
- 2 tbsp (30g) granulated erythritol
- 1/4 tsp (1g) salt

For the filling:
- 24 oz (680g) plain Greek yogurt (full fat)
- 16 oz (450g) cream cheese, softened
- 3 large eggs
- 2/3 cup (130g) granulated erythritol
- 1 tbsp (15ml) lemon juice
- 1 tsp (5ml) vanilla extract
- 1/4 tsp (1g) salt

INSTRUCTIONS

1. Preheat the oven to 325°F (165°C). Grease a 9-inch springform pan.
2. For the crust: In a medium bowl, mix almond flour, melted butter, erythritol, and salt until well combined.
3. Press the mixture firmly into the bottom of the prepared springform pan. Bake for 10 minutes, then remove from oven and let cool while preparing the filling.
4. For the filling: In a large bowl, beat cream cheese until smooth.
5. Add Greek yogurt, erythritol, lemon juice, vanilla extract, and salt. Beat until well combined.
6. Add eggs one at a time, beating on low speed just until combined. not overmix.
7. Pour the filling over the cooled crust.
8. Bake for 45-50 minutes, or until the center is almost set (it should jiggle slightly when the pan is tapped).
9. Turn off the oven and leave the cheesecake inside with the door closed for 1 hour.
10. Remove from the oven and run a knife around the rim of the pan to loosen the cheesecake. Let cool completely at room temperature.
11. Refrigerate for at least 4 hours or overnight before serving.

BERRY AND CHIA SEED PARFAIT

NUTRITIONAL VALUES (PER SERVING)
Calories: 180 *Carbohydrates:* 20g *Fiber:* 8g *Sugars:* 8g *Protein:* 9g *Fat:* 9g

PREP TIME
10 minutes

CHILL TIME
4 hours

SERVINGS
4
(1 parfait)

Storage Tip: These parfaits can be prepared in advance and stored in the refrigerator for up to 2 days. Add the sliced almonds just before serving to maintain their crunch.

INGREDIENTS

For the chia pudding:
1/4 cup (40g) chia seeds
1 cup (240ml) unsweetened almond milk
1 tsp (5ml) vanilla extract
2 tbsp (30ml) sugar-free maple syrup

For the berry compote:
2 cups (300g) mixed berries (strawberries, blueberries, raspberries)
2 tbsp (30ml) water
1 tbsp (15ml) lemon juice
1 tsp (5g) granulated erythritol (optional)

For assembly:
1 cup (240g) plain Greek yogurt (2% fat)
1/4 cup (30g) sliced almonds

INSTRUCTIONS

1. For the chia pudding: In a medium bowl, whisk together chia seeds, almond milk, vanilla extract, and sugar-free maple syrup.
2. Cover and refrigerate for at least 4 hours or overnight, stirring occasionally to prevent clumping.
3. For the berry compote: In a small saucepan, combine mixed berries, water, lemon juice, and erythritol (if using).
4. Bring to a simmer over medium heat, then reduce heat to low and cook for about 5-7 minutes, stirring occasionally, until berries have broken down slightly and the mixture has thickened.
5. Remove from heat and let cool completely. Refrigerate until ready to use.
6. To assemble the parfaits: In each of 4 glasses or jars, layer the ingredients as follows:
7. 2 tablespoons chia pudding
8. 2 tablespoons Greek yogurt
9. 2 tablespoons berry compote
10. Repeat layers
11. Top each parfait with 1 tablespoon sliced almonds.
12. Serve immediately or cover and refrigerate for up to 24 hours before serving.

COCONUT FLOUR CHOCOLATE CHIP COOKIES

NUTRITIONAL VALUES (PER SERVING)
Calories: 110 *Carbohydrates:* 8g *Fiber:* 3g *Sugars:* 2g *Protein:* 3g *Fat:* 8g

Storage Tip: Store in an airtight container at room temperature for up to 3 days, or in the refrigerator for up to a week. These cookies can also be frozen for up to 3 months.

PREP TIME
15 minutes

COOK TIME
12-15 minutes

SERVINGS
12
(cookie)

INGREDIENTS

1/2 cup (56g) coconut flour
1/4 cup (60ml) melted coconut oil
1/4 cup (60ml) sugar-free maple syrup
2 large eggs, room temperature
1 tsp (5ml) vanilla extract
1/4 tsp (1.5g) salt
1/4 tsp (1g) baking soda
1/3 cup (60g) sugar-free chocolate chips

INSTRUCTIONS

1. Preheat the oven to 350ºF (175ºC). Line a baking sheet with parchment paper.
2. In a large bowl, whisk together the melted coconut oil, sugar-free maple syrup, eggs, and vanilla extract until well combined.
3. In a separate bowl, mix the coconut flour, salt, and baking soda.
4. Add the dry ingredients to the wet ingredients and mix until a dough forms. The dough will be thick and somewhat sticky.
5. Fold in the sugar-free chocolate chips.
6. Using a cookie scoop or spoon, drop the dough onto the prepared baking sheet, making 12 cookies. Gently flatten each cookie with the palm of your hand or the back of a spoon, as they won't spread much during baking.
7. Bake for 12-15 minutes, or until the edges are golden brown.
8. Remove from the oven and let cool on the baking sheet for 5 minutes before transferring to a wire rack to cool completely.

ALMOND FLOUR RASPBERRY MUFFINS

NUTRITIONAL VALUES (PER SERVING)

Calories: 180 *Carbohydrates:* 9g *Fiber:* 3g *Sugars:* 3g *Protein:* 6g *Fat:* 14g

PREP TIME
15
minutes

COOK TIME
20-25
minutes

SERVINGS
12
(1 muffin)

Storage Tip: Store in an airtight container at room temperature for up to 2 days, or in the refrigerator for up to a week. These muffins can also be frozen for up to 3 months. Thaw at room temperature or reheat in the microwave for 15-20 seconds before serving.

INGREDIENTS

- 2 1/2 cups (280g) almond flour
- 1/4 cup (30g) coconut flour
- 1/2 cup (96g) granulated erythritol
- 2 tsp (10g) baking powder
- 1/4 tsp (1.5g) salt
- 1/4 cup (60ml) unsweetened almond milk
- 1/4 cup (60ml) melted coconut oil
- 3 large eggs
- 1 tsp (5ml) vanilla extract
- 1 tsp (5ml) almond extract
- 1 cup (125g) fresh raspberries

INSTRUCTIONS

1. Preheat the oven to 350°F (175°C). Line a 12-cup muffin tin with paper liners or grease with cooking spray.
2. In a large bowl, whisk together almond flour, coconut flour, erythritol, baking powder, and salt.
3. In a separate bowl, whisk together almond milk, melted coconut oil, eggs, vanilla extract, and almond extract.
4. Pour the wet ingredients into the dry ingredients and mix until well combined.
5. Gently fold in the raspberries, being careful not to crush them.
6. Divide the batter evenly among the prepared muffin cups, filling each about 2/3 full.
7. Bake for 20-25 minutes, or until a toothpick inserted into the center of a muffin comes out clean and the tops are golden brown.
8. Remove from the oven and let cool in the tin for 5 minutes.
9. Transfer muffins to a wire rack to cool completely.

SUGAR-FREE PEANUT BUTTER CUPS

NUTRITIONAL VALUES (PER SERVING)

Calories: 130 *Carbohydrates:* 7g *Fiber:* 3g *Sugars:* 1g *Protein:* 4g *Fat:* 11g

Storage Tip: Store in an airtight container in the refrigerator for up to 2 weeks, or in the freezer for up to 3 months. If frozen, let thaw at room temperature for about 10 minutes before enjoying.

PREP TIME
20
minutes

CHILL TIME
2 hours

SERVINGS
12
(1 peanut
butter cup)

INGREDIENTS

For the chocolate coating:
- 1 cup (170g) sugar-free dark chocolate chips
- 1 tbsp (15ml) coconut oil

For the peanut butter filling:
- 1/2 cup (128g) natural peanut butter (no added sugar)
- 2 tbsp (24g) powdered erythritol
- 1 tbsp (15ml) coconut flour
- 1/4 tsp (1.5g) salt

INSTRUCTIONS

1. Line a 12-cup muffin tin with paper liners.
2. In a microwave-safe bowl, combine the sugar-free chocolate chips and coconut oil. Microwave in 30-second intervals, stirring between each, until completely melted and smooth.
3. Spoon about 1 teaspoon of melted chocolate into each muffin liner, using the back of the spoon to spread it up the sides slightly. Place the muffin tin in the freezer for 10 minutes to set.
4. Meanwhile, in a medium bowl, mix together the peanut butter, powdered erythritol, coconut flour, and salt until well combined.
5. Remove the muffin tin from the freezer. Place about 1 tablespoon of the peanut butter mixture into each cup, gently pressing it down to flatten.
6. Top each cup with the remaining melted chocolate, making sure to cover the peanut butter completely.
7. Gently tap the muffin tin on the counter to remove any air bubbles and smooth out the chocolate.
8. Refrigerate for at least 2 hours or until the chocolate is completely set.
9. Once set, carefully remove the peanut butter cups from the paper liners before serving.

GRILLED PEACHES WITH RICOTTA AND HONEY

NUTRITIONAL VALUES (PER SERVING)

Calories: 120 *Carbohydrates:* 15g *Fiber:* 2g *Sugars:* 12g *Protein:* 5g *Fat:* 5g

PREP TIME
15 minutes

COOK TIME
6-8 minutes

SERVINGS
4
(1 peach half)

Storage Tip: This dish is best served immediately after preparation. If needed, grilled peaches can be stored separately in an airtight container in the refrigerator for up to 2 days. Reheat gently before assembling with the ricotta mixture.

INGREDIENTS

- 2 medium ripe peaches, halved and pitted
- tsp (5ml) olive oil
- 1/2 cup (120g) part-skim ricotta cheese
- 2 tbsp (30ml) honey
- 1/4 cup (30g) chopped pistachios
- 1/4 tsp ground cinnamon
- Fresh mint leaves for garnish (optional)

INSTRUCTIONS

1. Preheat a grill or grill pan over medium-high heat.
2. Brush the cut sides of the peaches lightly with olive oil to prevent sticking.
3. Place the peaches cut-side down on the grill. Grill for 3-4 minutes, or until grill marks appear and the peaches are slightly softened.
4. Flip the peaches and grill for an additional 2-3 minutes on the skin side.
5. Remove the peaches from the grill and let them cool slightly.
6. In a small bowl, mix the ricotta cheese with half of the honey (1 tbsp) and the cinnamon.
7. Divide the ricotta mixture among the four peach halves, spooning it into the center where the pit was.
8. Drizzle the remaining honey (1 tbsp) over the peaches and ricotta.
9. Sprinkle the chopped pistachios over each peach half.
10. If desired, garnish with fresh mint leaves.
11. Serve immediately while still warm.
12.
13. Tip: For a lower sugar option, you can reduce the honey to 1 tablespoon total or use a sugar-free honey alternative. The natural sweetness of the peaches and the creaminess of the ricotta will still provide plenty of flavor.

PUMPKIN SPICE CHIA PUDDING

NUTRITIONAL VALUES (PER SERVING)

Calories: 150 *Carbohydrates:* 15g *Fiber:* 8g *Sugars:* 5g *Protein:* 5g *Fat:* 9g

Storage Tip: This chia pudding can be stored in an airtight container in the refrigerator for up to 5 days. The texture may thicken over time; simply stir in a little almond milk if needed before serving.

PREP TIME
10 minutes

CHILL TIME
4h or overnight

SERVINGS
4
(1/2 cup)

INGREDIENTS

- 1/4 cup (40g) chia seeds
- cup (240ml) unsweetened almond milk
- 1/2 cup (120g) canned pumpkin puree (not pumpkin pie filling)
- tbsp (30ml) sugar-free maple syrup or to taste
- tsp (5ml) vanilla extract
- tsp (2g) pumpkin pie spice
- 1/4 tsp (1g) ground cinnamon
- nch of salt

* optional toppings:*
- chopped pecans
- strawberries cut in half
- tbsp (60g) sugar-free whipped cream

INSTRUCTIONS

1. In a medium bowl, whisk together the chia seeds, almond milk, pumpkin puree, sugar-free maple syrup, vanilla extract, pumpkin pie spice, cinnamon, and salt until well combined.
2. Cover the bowl with plastic wrap or transfer the mixture to a container with a lid.
3. Refrigerate for at least 4 hours or overnight, stirring occasionally during the first hour to prevent clumping.
4. Once the pudding has thickened, give it a good stir. If it's too thick, add a little more almond milk. If it's too thin, add more chia seeds and let it sit for another 30 minutes.
5. Taste and adjust sweetness if needed by adding more sugar-free maple syrup.
6. Divide the pudding evenly among 4 serving bowls or glasses.
7. If desired, top each serving with 1 tablespoon of chopped pecans and 1 tablespoon of sugar-free whipped cream.
8. Serve chilled.

SUGAR-FREE LEMON BARS WITH ALMOND CRUST

NUTRITIONAL VALUES (PER SERVING)

Calories: 120 *Carbohydrates:* 6g *Fiber:* 2g *Sugars:* 1g *Protein:* 4g *Fat:* 10g

PREP TIME
20 minutes

COOK TIME
35m (+2h CHILL TIME)

SERVINGS
16 (1 bar)

Storage Tip: Store in an airtight container in the refrigerator for up to 5 days. These bars can also be frozen for up to 3 months. Thaw in the refrigerator before serving.

INGREDIENTS

For the crust:
- 2 cups (224g) almond flour
- 1/4 cup (48g) granulated erythritol
- 1/4 tsp salt
- 1/4 cup (56g) unsalted butter, melted

For the lemon filling:
- 4 large eggs
- 1/2 cup (96g) granulated erythritol
- 1/4 cup (48g) powdered erythritol
- 1/2 cup (120ml) fresh lemon juice (about 4 lemons)
- 2 tbsp (14g) coconut flour
- 1 tbsp lemon zest
- 1/4 tsp salt

Optional:
- Additional powdered erythritol for dusting

INSTRUCTIONS

1. Preheat the oven to 350°F (175°C). Line an 8x8 inch baking pan with parchment paper, leaving some overhang for easy removal.
2. For the crust: In a medium bowl, mix together almond flour, 1/4 cup granulated erythritol, and 1/4 tsp salt. Add melted butter and mix unt a crumbly dough forms.
3. Press the dough evenly into the bottom of the prepared pan. Bake fc 15-18 minutes, until lightly golden. Remove from oven and let cool slightly.
4. For the filling: In a large bowl, whisk together eggs, 1/2 cup granulatec erythritol, and powdered erythritol until smooth.
5. Add lemon juice, coconut flour, lemon zest, and 1/4 tsp salt. Whisk un well combined and no lumps remain.
6. Pour the filling over the pre-baked crust.
7. Return the pan to the oven and bake for 20-22 minutes, or until the filling is set but still slightly jiggly in the center.
8. Remove from the oven and let cool completely at room temperatur
9. Once cooled, refrigerate for at least 2 hours or overnight to fully set.
10. Use the parchment paper overhang to lift the bars out of the pan. C into 16 squares.
11. If desired, dust with additional powdered erythritol before serving.

SUGAR-FREE CHOCOLATE BROWNIES

NUTRITIONAL VALUES (PER SERVING)

Calories: 140 *Carbohydrates:* 7g *Fiber:* 3g *Sugars:* 1g *Protein:* 5g *Fat:* 12g

Storage Tip: Store in an airtight container at room temperature for up to 3 days, or in the refrigerator for up to a week. These brownies can also be frozen for up to 3 months. Thaw at room temperature before serving.

PREP TIME
15 minutes

CHILL TIME
25-30m (+1 hour CHILL TIME)

SERVINGS
16 (1 brownie)

INGREDIENTS

- 1 cup (112g) almond flour
- 1/2 cup (48g) unsweetened cocoa powder
- 3/4 cup (144g) granulated erythritol
- 1/2 tsp baking powder
- 1/4 tsp salt
- 1/2 cup (112g) unsalted butter, melted
- 2 large eggs
- 1 tsp vanilla extract
- 1/4 cup (60ml) unsweetened almond milk
- 1/3 cup (57g) sugar-free dark chocolate chips
- 1/4 cup (28g) chopped walnuts (optional)
- 1/4 cup (28g) berries for decoration (optional)

INSTRUCTIONS

1. Preheat the oven to 350°F (175°C). Line an 8x8 inch baking pan with parchment paper, leaving some overhang for easy removal.
2. In a medium bowl, whisk together almond flour, cocoa powder, erythritol, baking powder, and salt.
3. In a large bowl, whisk together melted butter, eggs, vanilla extract, c almond milk until well combined.
4. Gradually add the dry ingredients to the wet ingredients, stirring un just combined. The batter will be thick.
5. Fold in the sugar-free chocolate chips and chopped walnuts (if usi
6. Spread the batter evenly in the prepared pan.
7. Bake for 25-30 minutes, or until a toothpick inserted into the center comes out with a few moist crumbs. Be careful not to overbake, as brownies will continue to set as they cool.
8. Remove from the oven and let cool in the pan for about 1 hour.
9. Use the parchment paper overhang to lift the brownies out of the Cut into 16 squares.

These recipes show you can eat well with diabetes without bland food or complex cooking. Use them as a starting point and adjust to your tastes. **The goal is simple: balance nutrients and keep your blood sugar steady.** With time, making these meals will become routine.

Feel free to experiment, but stick to the principles we've covered. Enjoying your food matters—it helps you stay on track.

EXTRA BONUS:

ACCESS 20 DIABETES-FRIENDLY VIDEO RECIPES

Managing meal planning and special occasions with diabetes can seem challenging, but with the right strategies, it's entirely manageable. To make your journey even easier, **we're excited to offer you access to 20 easy-to-follow video recipes tailored for diabetes management**. These recipes can help you prepare delicious, balanced meals for everyday eating and special occasions alike.

Simply scan the QR code provided in this chapter to unlock this valuable resource. Whether you're looking for quick weekday dinners, holiday-friendly dishes, or tasty options for dining with family and friends, **these video recipes will inspire you to create meals that are both satisfying and supportive of your health goals**. Don't miss out on this opportunity to expand your diabetes-friendly recipe collection—scan the QR code now and start exploring these helpful video tutorials!

*****

Next up, we'll look at lifestyle tips that work alongside your diet to manage diabetes better.

5. LIFESTYLE TIPS FOR MANAGING DIABETES

Managing diabetes goes beyond just watching what you eat. This chapter covers key lifestyle changes that can make a big difference in your health and quality of life.

We'll explore five main areas:

1. **Exercise:** How regular physical activity can help control your blood sugar and improve your overall health.

2. **Stress management:** Techniques to reduce stress—stress can affect your blood sugar levels and make diabetes harder to manage.

3. **Regular check-ups:** The importance of staying on top of your health with routine medical visits and tests.

4. **Staying motivated:** Strategies to keep you on track with your diabetes management plan, even when it gets tough.

5. **Building a support system:** How to create a network of people who can help you manage your diabetes effectively.

These lifestyle changes might seem small, but they can have a big impact on your health. I believe the practical, actionable tips in this chapter will help you to better manage your diabetes and improve your overall well-being. Start using them right away!

These lifestyle changes are about creating habits that you can maintain long-term. Let's explore how you can take control of your health beyond just your diet.

THE ROLE OF EXERCISE

Exercise is necessary for managing diabetes, especially as you age. It's not just about losing weight—it's about controlling your blood sugar, improving your heart health, and feeling better overall.

BENEFITS OF EXERCISE FOR DIABETES MANAGEMENT

Exercise plays a crucial role in diabetes management, offering a wide array of benefits that contribute to overall health and well-being. Regular physical activity has been shown to effectively lower blood sugar levels, providing immediate and long-term improvements in glucose control. Additionally, exercise enhances insulin sensitivity, allowing your body to use insulin more efficiently, which is particularly beneficial for those with type 2 diabetes. Maintaining a healthy weight becomes easier with consistent exercise, reducing the strain on your body and helping to prevent complications associated with diabetes. Furthermore, engaging in **regular physical activity significantly reduces the risk of heart disease**, a common concern for individuals with diabetes. Beyond these physiological benefits, exercise also provides a substantial boost to mood and energy levels, contributing to an improved quality of life.

HOW EXERCISE CONTROLS BLOOD SUGAR

The mechanism by which exercise controls blood sugar is multifaceted. During physical activity, your muscles use glucose for energy, effectively lowering blood sugar levels. This process continues even after you've finished exercising, as your body replenishes its energy stores. Moreover, physical activity increases your body's sensitivity to insulin, allowing it to work more effectively in moving glucose from your bloodstream into your cells. Over time, consistent exercise can lead to a noticeable reduction in your A1C levels, a key indicator of long-term blood sugar control.

IMPORTANCE OF CARDIOVASCULAR HEALTH

For persons with diabetes, maintaining **cardiovascular health is of utmost importance.** Diabetes significantly increases the risk of heart disease, making it crucial to engage in activities that strengthen the heart and blood vessels. Cardiovascular exercise, such as brisk walking, swimming, or cycling, plays a vital role in achieving this. Regular **cardio workouts** not only strengthen your heart but also **help control blood pressure** and **cholesterol levels**, further reducing your risk of cardiovascular complications.

TIPS FOR INCORPORATING EXERCISE INTO DAILY ROUTINES

Incorporating exercise into your daily routine doesn't have to be daunting. Let's explore some tips to help you incorporate it:

- Start small, remembering that even 10 minutes of activity a day can make a significant difference.

- Choose activities you enjoy, as this increases the likelihood of sticking with your exercise plan. Walking, swimming, and dancing are all excellent options that provide cardiovascular benefits while being gentle on the joints.

- Look for opportunities to increase activity in your everyday life, such as taking the stairs instead of the elevator or parking farther from store entrances.

- Joining a group class, particularly those focused on seniors, can provide motivation and social interaction. Many community centers offer programs tailored to older adults with various fitness levels.

- Aim for consistency in your exercise routine, working towards 30 minutes of moderate activity most days of the week.

The key to reaping the benefits of exercise for diabetes management lies in making it a regular part of your lifestyle.

Talk to your doctor before starting any new exercise routine. They can help you create a plan that's safe and effective for your specific needs.

Don't let age or physical limitations stop you. There's always a way to be more active, even if it's chair exercises or gentle stretching. The key is to move more and sit less.

To further explore exercise strategies for diabetes management, **we've prepared a comprehensive guide: Move More, Stress Less: Exercise Guide for Diabetes Management.** This free ebook offers a range of low-impact exercises tailored for seniors with diabetes, along with detailed explanations of how each exercise benefits your blood sugar control and overall health.

STRESS MANAGEMENT AND DIABETES

Stress isn't only unpleasant—**it can also directly affect your blood sugar levels** and make diabetes harder to manage. Let's look at why stress matters and what you can do about it.

Living with diabetes requires careful management of many different aspects of your health. One factor that's often overlooked is the significant impact of stress. Stress, whether acute or chronic, can have significant effects on your ability to manage diabetes effectively.

From influencing blood sugar levels directly to altering your daily habits, stress can create a multitude of challenges for persons with diabetes. Understanding this connection is necessary for developing a comprehensive approach to your diabetes care that addresses both physical and emotional well-being. Let's explore how stress affects diabetes management and why it's important to incorporate stress-reduction techniques into your overall diabetes care plan.

IMPACT OF STRESS ON DIABETES MANAGEMENT

Stress significantly affects diabetes management in various ways. When you're under stress, your body releases hormones like cortisol and adrenaline, which can cause your blood sugar levels to rise. This physiological response can make it more challenging to maintain stable glucose levels.

Stress often leads to unhealthy eating habits, such as emotional eating or skipping meals, both of which can disrupt your blood sugar balance. In times of high stress, you might find yourself neglecting your diabetes care routine, perhaps forgetting to check your blood sugar regularly or taking medications as prescribed.

Stress frequently interferes with sleep patterns, and poor sleep quality can further complicate blood sugar control. The relationship between stress and diabetes is cyclical – stress can worsen diabetes symptoms, and the challenges of managing diabetes can, in turn, increase stress levels.

IMPORTANCE OF MENTAL HEALTH

Mental health plays a crucial role in overall well-being, especially for individuals managing diabetes. There's a close, bidirectional relationship between mental and physical health—each significantly influences the other.

People with diabetes are at a higher risk of developing mental health conditions such as depression and anxiety. These conditions can make it more difficult to adhere to diabetes management routines, potentially leading to poorer health outcomes.

Maintaining good mental health can greatly improve your ability to manage diabetes effectively. When you're in a positive mental state, you're more likely to have the energy and motivation to stick to your treatment plan, make healthy lifestyle choices, and actively engage in self-care.

Recognizing the importance of mental health in diabetes management, healthcare providers increasingly emphasize a holistic approach that addresses both physical and psychological aspects of living with diabetes.

TECHNIQUES FOR MANAGING STRESS

Managing stress is crucial for effective diabetes control, and there are several techniques you can employ to reduce stress levels and improve your overall well-being.

Deep Breathing

Take a few minutes each day to practice slow, deep breaths. Inhale deeply through your nose for a count of four, hold for a count of four, then exhale slowly through your mouth for a count of six. This practice can help lower your heart rate and blood pressure, promoting a sense of calm and reducing the physiological effects of stress on your body.

Progressive Muscle Relaxation

Progressive muscle relaxation is another effective method for stress relief. This technique involves systematically tensing and then relaxing each muscle group in your body. Start with your toes and work your way up to your head. Tense each muscle group for about five seconds, then release and relax for 30 seconds. This practice not only helps reduce physical tension but also encourages mental relaxation.

Guided Imagery

This is a form of mental escape that can significantly lower stress levels. Find a quiet place and close your eyes. Visualize a calm, peaceful scene in vivid detail – perhaps a serene beach or a tranquil forest. Engage all your senses in this visualization: imagine the sounds, smells, and physical sensations of being in this peaceful place. This technique can help distract your mind from stressors and promote a state of relaxation.

Physical Activity

Even a short walk can help reduce stress hormones and improve your mood. Aim for at least 30 minutes of moderate exercise most days of the week. This could be brisk walking, swimming, cycling, or any activity you enjoy. Regular exercise not only helps manage stress but also improves blood sugar control and overall health.

Engaging in Hobbies

Engaging in hobbies is an excellent way to manage stress and improve your quality of life. Dedicate time to activities you enjoy, whether it's gardening, painting, reading, or playing a musical instrument. Hobbies provide a sense of accomplishment and joy, helping to counteract the effects of stress. They also offer a healthy distraction from diabetes-related worries and can be a form of mindfulness, keeping you focused on the present moment.

Different stress-management techniques work for different people. Experiment with these methods to find what works best for you, and consider adding a combination of these techniques into your daily routine for optimal stress reduction and diabetes management.

MINDFULNESS AND MEDITATION

Mindfulness and meditation are skills that develop over time. Be patient with yourself as you begin this practice, and don't be discouraged if your mind wanders –that's completely normal. The goal is to gently bring your attention back to the present moment whenever you notice your mind has drifted.

Understanding Mindfulness

Mindfulness means paying attention to the present moment without judgment. It involves being fully aware of your thoughts, feelings, bodily sensations, and surrounding environment. This practice can help you become more attuned to your body's signals, including changes in blood sugar levels, hunger, or stress responses. By cultivating mindfulness, you may better manage your diabetes by making more conscious choices about food, exercise, and self-care.

Benefits of Diabetes Management

Practicing mindfulness and meditation can help reduce anxiety and improve mood, which is particularly beneficial for those managing diabetes. These techniques can lower stress hormones that may affect blood sugar levels. Additionally, mindfulness can enhance your ability to stick to your diabetes management plan by increasing self-awareness and self-control.

Getting Started

Begin with just a few minutes of mindfulness or meditation each day. You can start by simply focusing on your breath for 2-3 minutes. Gradually increase the duration as you become more comfortable with the practice. Consistency is more important than length, so aim to practice daily, even if it's just for a short time.

Guided Resources

If you're new to meditation, consider using apps or guided recordings to help you get started. Many free and paid apps offer guided meditations specifically designed for beginners. These resources can provide structure and guidance as you develop your mindfulness practice. Some popular options include Headspace, Calm, and Insight Timer, which offer a variety of guided meditations and mindfulness exercises.

Incorporating Mindfulness into Daily Life

Beyond formal meditation sessions, try to incorporate mindfulness into your daily activities. This could include eating mindfully by paying attention to the flavors and textures of your food or practicing mindful walking by focusing on the sensation of your feet touching the ground. These small moments of mindfulness throughout the day can accumulate to have a significant positive impact on your stress levels and overall well-being.

TIPS FOR INCORPORATING STRESS MANAGEMENT INTO DAILY LIFE

- Set aside **specific times** for relaxation each day
- **Start small**—even 5 minutes can make a difference
- **Make it a routine,** like brushing your teeth
- Try different techniques to find what works best for you
- Consider joining a **stress management class or support group**

Managing stress is a skill that takes practice. Don't get discouraged if you don't see immediate results. These techniques can significantly improve your ability to handle stress and manage your diabetes more effectively.

If you're feeling overwhelmed or struggling with stress, don't hesitate to talk to your healthcare provider. They can offer additional resources or refer you to a mental health professional if needed.

IMPORTANCE OF REGULAR CHECK-UPS

Regular check-ups are crucial for managing diabetes effectively. They help catch problems early and keep your health on track by:

- monitoring **blood sugar control**
- **detecting** complications **early**
- adjusting **treatment plan** as needed
- **answering your questions** and concerns

WHAT TO EXPECT DURING CHECK-UPS

Regular check-ups are an important part of managing diabetes effectively. These appointments provide an opportunity for your healthcare provider to monitor your overall health and make necessary adjustments to your treatment plan. Here's what you can typically expect during these check-ups:

Blood Pressure Measurement

Your healthcare provider will measure your **blood pressure** at each visit. This is important because people with diabetes are at higher risk for hypertension, which can lead to cardiovascular complications. Your doctor will work with you to keep your blood pressure within a healthy range, typically below 140/90 mmHg for most adults with diabetes.

Weight Check

Your **weight** will be recorded at each visit. Maintaining a healthy weight is crucial for managing diabetes, as excess weight can increase insulin resistance. Your healthcare provider may discuss strategies for weight management if needed, including dietary changes and exercise recommendations.

Foot Examination

A thorough **foot examination** is typically conducted at least once a year, or more frequently if you have a history of foot problems. This exam checks for signs of neuropathy (nerve damage), poor circulation, and other foot-related issues that are common in people with diabetes.

Review of Blood Sugar Logs

Your healthcare provider will review your **blood sugar logs** to assess how well your current treatment plan is working. This review helps identify patterns and trends in your blood glucose levels, which can inform decisions about adjusting your medication, diet, or exercise regimen.

Discussion of Symptoms or Concerns

Your check-up is an opportunity to discuss any new **symptoms** or concerns you may have. This could include changes in your vision, unusual sensations in your extremities, difficulties with medication management, or any other diabetes-related issues you're experiencing.

IMPORTANT TESTS AND SCREENINGS

In addition to regular check-ups, several important tests and screenings are crucial for comprehensive diabetes management (American Diabetes Association, 2021):

A1C Test

The **A1C test** measures your average blood sugar level over the past 2-3 months. It's typically performed 2-4 times a year. Your healthcare provider will use this information to assess how well your diabetes is being controlled and whether any changes to your treatment plan are necessary.

Cholesterol Test

An annual **cholesterol test** is important because diabetes increases your risk of cardiovascular disease. This test measures your LDL ("bad") cholesterol, HDL ("good") cholesterol, and triglycerides. Your healthcare provider may recommend more frequent testing if your levels are not within the target range.

Kidney Function Tests

Annual **kidney function tests** are crucial for detecting early signs of diabetic kidney disease. These tests typically include a urine test to check for albumin (a protein that can indicate kidney damage) and a blood test to measure creatinine levels.

Eye Exam

An annual comprehensive **eye exam** is essential for detecting and monitoring diabetic retinopathy, a common complication of diabetes that affects the eyes. This exam typically includes dilation of your pupils to allow for a thorough examination of your retina.

Dental Check-ups

Regular **dental check-ups**, ideally twice a year, are important because diabetes can increase your risk of gum disease. Your dentist will check for signs of gum disease and provide guidance on maintaining good oral hygiene.

PREPARING FOR MEDICAL APPOINTMENTS

To make the most of your medical appointments, consider the following preparation steps:

BRING YOUR BLOOD SUGAR LOGS

Bring your blood sugar logs or glucose meter to your appointment. This information helps your healthcare provider understand your day-to-day glucose control.

LIST ANY NEW SYMPTOMS OR CONCERNS

Make a list of any new **symptoms**, concerns, or questions you have. This ensures you don't forget to discuss important issues during your appointment.

BRING ALL YOUR MEDICATIONS

Bring all your current **medications**, including over-the-counter drugs and supplements. This helps your healthcare provider identify any potential drug interactions or side effects.

WRITE DOWN QUESTIONS BEFOREHAND

Prepare a list of questions you want to ask your healthcare provider. This might include questions about your treatment plan, lifestyle modifications, or any new diabetes research you've heard about.

CONSIDER BRINGING A FAMILY MEMBER OR FRIEND

Having a **support** person with you can be helpful. They can take notes, ask questions you might forget, and help you remember the information provided during the appointment.

ROLE OF HEALTHCARE PROVIDERS

Your healthcare team plays a vital role in your diabetes management:

INTERPRET TEST RESULTS

Your healthcare provider will interpret the results of your various tests and screenings, explaining what they mean for your overall health and diabetes management.

ADJUST MEDICATIONS IF NEEDED

Based on your **test results** and symptoms, your healthcare provider may adjust your medications. This could involve changing dosages, adding new medications, or discontinuing others.

PROVIDE EDUCATION AND SUPPORT

Your **healthcare team** is a valuable source of education and support. They can provide information on the latest diabetes management techniques, offer guidance on lifestyle modifications, and help you navigate the challenges of living with diabetes.

REFER TO SPECIALISTS WHEN NECESSARY

If needed, your primary healthcare provider may refer you to specialists such as endocrinologists, ophthalmologists, or nephrologists for more specialized care.

Effective diabetes management is a joint effort between you and your healthcare team. Actively participate in your care and maintain open communication with your providers to achieve better control of your diabetes and improve your overall health outcomes.

QUITTING SMOKING: AN IMPORTANT STEP IN DIABETES MANAGEMENT

If you're a smoker with diabetes, quitting is one of the most important steps you can take for your health. Smoking and diabetes are a dangerous combination that significantly increases your risk of serious health complications.

WHY QUITTING MATTERS FOR DIABETES MANAGEMENT

- **Improves insulin sensitivity** and blood sugar control
- **Reduces risk of heart disease** and stroke
- Lowers risk of kidney disease and nerve damage
- **Improves circulation**, especially in the feet and legs
- **Decreases risk of eye problems** and vision loss

CHALLENGES OF QUITTING

- Nicotine is highly addictive
- Smoking may be a long-standing habit

- Concerns about weight gain

STRATEGIES FOR QUITTING

1. Talk to your doctor about **nicotine replacement** therapy or medications
2. **Set a quit date** and stick to it
3. Identify your smoking **triggers** and plan alternatives
4. Seek **support** from family, friends, or support groups
5. **Stay physically active** to manage stress and potential weight gain
6. **Be patient** with yourself - quitting often takes several attempts

It's never too late to quit. The benefits of quitting smoking begin almost immediately and continue to grow over time. Even if you've smoked for years, quitting now can still improve your health and diabetes management.

If you're a smoker, quitting is one of the most impactful steps you can take for your health when managing diabetes.

Our free ebook, Breathe Easy: A Guide to Quitting Smoking for People with Diabetes, offers targeted strategies and information about the specific benefits of quitting for people with diabetes. It's a valuable resource to support you in taking this important step for your health. Scan the QR code below to access and download this guide:

Your healthcare team can provide additional resources and support to help you quit smoking. Don't hesitate to ask for help - quitting

smoking is a challenge, but it's one that can dramatically improve your health and quality of life with diabetes.

STAYING MOTIVATED AND CONSISTENT

Staying motivated on your journey with diabetes is important for long-term success.

IMPORTANCE OF MOTIVATION AND CONSISTENCY

Motivation and **consistency** are key pillars in effective diabetes management, significantly impacting both immediate and long-term health outcomes. When you maintain a consistent approach to your diabetes care and stay motivated to adhere to your treatment plan, you're more likely to achieve better blood sugar control. This improved control isn't just about numbers; it translates into feeling better day-to-day, with more energy and fewer symptoms like fatigue or mood swings.

This consistent management leads to a reduced risk of diabetes-related complications such as heart disease, kidney problems, and nerve damage. The habits formed through consistent care – regular exercise, healthy eating, and proper medication management – contribute to an overall healthier lifestyle.

This improves your quality of life in numerous ways, allowing you to more fully participate in activities you enjoy and maintain better mental health. While staying motivated can be challenging at times, remembering these significant benefits can help you stay on track. Each day of consistent management is an investment in your future health and well-being, making the effort truly worthwhile.

SETTING REALISTIC GOALS

Starting on a journey to better health begins with setting achievable milestones that pave the way for lasting change.

- Start small and build up
- Make goals specific and measurable
- Set both short-term and long-term goals

TRACKING PROGRESS

Monitoring your journey provides you with valuable insights, helping you celebrate victories and identify areas for improvement in your diabetes management.

- Keep a **diabetes journal**
- Use apps or devices to monitor blood sugar
- Regularly review your progress with your healthcare team

CELEBRATING ACHIEVEMENTS

Recognizing your progress, no matter how small, reinforces positive habits and boosts motivation for continued success in managing your diabetes.

- Acknowledge small victories
- Reward yourself in healthy ways
- Share successes with friends and family

COMMON CHALLENGES AND SOLUTIONS

- Burnout: Take breaks, but don't give up
- Setbacks: Learn from them, don't dwell on them
- Lack of support: Join a diabetes support group

Greg, 68, struggled with motivation until he started setting small, weekly goals. He says, "I used to get overwhelmed thinking about managing diabetes forever. Now I focus on one week at a time. Last week, I walked 15 minutes every day. This week, I'm aiming for 20. These small wins keep me going."

Everyone's journey with diabetes is different. Find what motivates you and stick with it. It's okay to have off days—what matters is getting back on track.

BUILDING A SUPPORT SYSTEM

Managing diabetes isn't a solo journey. A strong **support system** can make a big difference in your success and well-being.

IMPORTANCE OF A SUPPORT SYSTEM

- Provides **emotional support**
- Helps with **practical tasks**
- **Encourages** you to stick to your management plan
- Reduces feelings of **isolation**

Role of Family and Friends

Building a support system takes time. Start small—maybe with one family member or friend. Gradually expand your network. Don't be afraid to ask for help when you need it. Most people are willing to support you if they know how.

Family and friends can:

- learn about diabetes to better understand your needs
- help with meal planning and preparation
- remind you about medications or doctor appointments
- join you in adopting healthier lifestyle habits

Community Support

Explore the following options:

- Local diabetes education programs
- Senior center activities focused on health
- Gym or fitness classes tailored for seniors
- Cooking classes for healthy eating

FINDING AND JOINING SUPPORT GROUPS

- Ask your healthcare provider for recommendations
- Check with local hospitals or community centers

- Look for online forums or social media groups
- Consider diabetes-specific organizations like the American Diabetes Association.

Your healthcare team is also part of your **support system**. Keep them informed about your challenges and successes. They can provide resources and adjust your care plan as needed.

Building a strong support system isn't just helpful - it can be enjoyable too. You might find new friends or strengthen existing relationships as you work together toward better health.

BENEFITS OF CONNECTING WITH OTHERS MANAGING DIABETES

Living with diabetes can sometimes feel isolating, but connecting with others who share similar experiences can be incredibly beneficial for your physical and emotional well-being. Here are some key advantages of building connections within the **diabetes community**:

SHARE TIPS AND STRATEGIES

Connecting with others who have diabetes provides an excellent opportunity to exchange practical advice and management strategies. Every person's journey with diabetes is unique, and you can learn valuable tips that you might not hear from your healthcare provider. For instance, someone might share their method for remembering to take medications, a trick for making finger pricks less painful, or a diabetes-friendly recipe they've discovered. These peer-to-peer exchanges can significantly enhance your day-to-day diabetes management.

LEARN FROM OTHERS' EXPERIENCES

When you interact with others managing diabetes, you gain insights from their experiences with different treatments, technologies, or lifestyle changes. Someone who has been living with diabetes for many years might offer perspective on long-term management, while someone newly diagnosed might share fresh coping strategies. Learning about others' successes and challenges can help you make more informed decisions about your own care and prepare you for potential hurdles you might face.

FIND MOTIVATION AND ENCOURAGEMENT

Managing a chronic condition like diabetes requires constant effort, and it's natural to sometimes feel overwhelmed or discouraged. Connecting with others who understand these challenges can provide much-needed motivation and encouragement. Seeing others successfully managing their diabetes can inspire you to stay committed to your own health goals. Moreover, on difficult days, having a supportive community to turn to can make a significant difference in maintaining a positive outlook.

REALIZE YOU'RE NOT ALONE IN YOUR CHALLENGES

One of the most powerful benefits of connecting with others managing diabetes is the realization that you're not alone in your struggles. Diabetes can present unique challenges that those without the condition might not fully understand. Sharing your experiences with others who "get it" can be incredibly validating and comforting. Whether it's frustration over fluctuating blood sugar levels or anxiety about long-term complications, knowing that others face similar challenges can help reduce feelings of isolation and stress.

ACCESS TO UP-TO-DATE INFORMATION

The diabetes community is often at the forefront of new developments in treatment and management. By connecting with others, you may learn about new research, emerging technologies, or clinical trials that could benefit your care. While it's important to always consult with your healthcare provider before making changes to your treatment plan, being part of an informed community can help you stay aware of potential options and advancements in diabetes care.

OPPORTUNITY FOR ADVOCACY AND AWARENESS

Connecting with others managing diabetes can also provide opportunities to get involved in advocacy efforts. Whether it's participating in diabetes awareness campaigns, fundraising for research, or advocating for better healthcare policies, being part of a community allows you to contribute to the broader cause of improving life for all people with diabetes.

While connecting with others can be incredibly beneficial, it's important to approach shared information critically and always consult with your healthcare provider before making significant changes to your diabetes management plan.

Throughout this chapter, we've explored key lifestyle factors that play a crucial role in managing diabetes beyond diet. From the importance of regular exercise and stress management to the value of consistent check-ups, staying motivated, and building a strong support system—each of these elements contributes to your overall health and well-being.

Managing diabetes is about creating a sustainable lifestyle that works for you. It's not about perfection, but about making consistent efforts to take care of yourself.

*****

As we move to **the conclusion of this book**, let's recap the main points and I'll provide you with find thoughts on living well with diabetes after 60.

CONCLUSION

Throughout this book, we've explored the many facets of managing diabetes after 60. From understanding the basics of diabetes to creating balanced meal plans, incorporating exercise, and managing stress—we've covered a lot of ground.

The key takeaway is this: diabetes management isn't just about controlling your blood sugar. It's about adopting a holistic approach that encompasses your diet, physical activity, mental health, and overall lifestyle.

YOU CAN DO THIS: REAFFIRMING THE CORE MESSAGE

If there's one thing I want you to remember, it's this: you can effectively manage your diabetes. It might seem overwhelming at times, but with the strategies we've discussed, you have the tools to take control of your health. Remember, it's not about perfection. It's about making consistent, sustainable choices that improve your quality of life.

TAKING ACTION: YOUR NEXT STEPS

Now that you have this information, it's time to put it into action. Start small—perhaps by incorporating one new diabetes-friendly recipe into your weekly meal plan, or by adding a 10-minute walk to your daily routine. Build on these small changes over time. Consistency is key.

STAY MOTIVATED AND KEEP LEARNING

Managing diabetes is an ongoing journey. As you implement these strategies, you'll learn what works best for you. Stay curious and open to adjusting your approach as needed. Every small step forward is a victory.

ADDITIONAL RESOURCES

To support your journey, we've prepared some additional resources:

- **Festive Feasts:** Diabetes-Friendly Recipes for Special Occasions —An ebook filled with low-GI recipes and menu plans for celebrations.
- **Move More, Stress Less:** Exercise Guide for Diabetes Management —This ebook offers low-impact exercises tailored for seniors with diabetes.
- **Breathe Easy:** A Guide to Quitting Smoking for People with Diabetes —Learn about the specific benefits of quitting smoking when you have diabetes, along with practical strategies to help you quit.

Access to 20 easy-to-follow video recipes tailored for diabetes management.

These resources are available for free download. They're designed to complement the information in this book and provide more in-depth guidance on specific aspects of diabetes management. Scan the QR code below for instant download:

YOUR FEEDBACK MATTERS

Your experience with this book is invaluable. If you've found it helpful, please consider leaving an honest review. Your feedback not only helps other readers but also assists us in improving future editions. We're committed to providing the most useful, up-to-date information to support you in your diabetes management journey.

You're not flying solo on this journey. With the right knowledge, support, and mindset, you can live a full, healthy life with diabetes. Here's to your health and well-being!

REFERENCES

Alarakha, S., & Sruthi, M. (n.d.). Low-Glycemic foods list guide. MedicineNet. https://www.medicinenet.com/low-glycemic_foods_list_guide/article.htm

American Diabetes Association. (2018). Classification and Diagnosis of Diabetes: Standards of Medical Care in Diabetes—2018. Diabetes Care, 41(Supplement 1), S13–S27. https://doi.org/10.2337/dc18-s002

American Diabetes Association. (2019). Understanding A1C. Diabetes.org. https://www.diabetes.org/a1c

American Diabetes Association. (2021). Introduction: Standards of medical care in diabetes—2022. Diabetes Care, 45(Supplement_1), S1–S2. https://doi.org/10.2337/dc22-sint

American Diabetes Association, & American Heart Association. (2018, July 19). Diabetes & heart healthy meals for two. https://www.heart.org/en/healthy-living/healthy-eating/eat-smart/aha-cookbooks/diabetes-and-heart-healthy-meals-for-two

Bauer, E. (2024, April 2). White bean and tuna salad. Simply Recipes. https://www.simplyrecipes.com/recipes/white_bean_and_tuna_salad/

Bennett, B. (2012, October 4). Naturally sweetened green protein smoothie. Sugarfreemom.com. https://www.sugarfreemom.com/recipes/naturally-sweetened-green-protein-smoothie/

Bennett, B. (2013, December 17). Homemade sugar-free peanut butter cups. Sugar Free Mom. https://www.sugarfreemom.com/recipes/homemade-sugar-free-peanut-butter-cups/

Bennett, B. (2014, April 17). Sugar-free chocolate brownies recipe. Sugarfreemom.com. https://www.sugarfreemom.com/recipes/sugar-free-chocolate-brownies-recipe/

Bryan, L. (2020, August 24). Mediterranean chickpea salad. Downshiftology. https://downshiftology.com/recipes/mediterranean-chickpea-salad/

Cauliflower rice burrito bowl. (2016, July 5). Minimalist Baker. https://minimalistbaker.com/cauliflower-rice-burrito-bowl/

Centers for Disease Control and Prevention. (2020a). National Diabetes Statistics Report, 2020. U.S. Dept of Health and Human Services.

Centers for Disease Control and Prevention. (2020b). National diabetes statistics report, 2020: Estimates of diabetes and its burden in the United States. United States Dept of Health and Human Services. https://stacks.cdc.gov/view/cdc/85309

Centers for Disease Control and Prevention. (2024a, May 13). About insulin resistance and type 2 diabetes. CDC. https://www.cdc.gov/diabetes/about/insulin-resistance-type-2-diabetes.html

Centers for Disease Control and Prevention. (2024b, May 13). Prediabetes—Your chance to prevent type 2 diabetes. CDC. https://www.cdc.gov/diabetes/prevention-type-2/prediabetes-pre-vent-type-2.html?CDC_AAref_Val=https://www.cdc.gov/diabetes/basics/prediabetes.html

Charles Alexis, A. (2022, February 15). 6 filling parfaits that won't spike your blood sugar. Healthline; Healthline Media. https://www.healthline.com/nutrition/6-filling-parfaits-that-wont-spike-your-blood-sugar#6.-Berry-parfait

Charvat, H., Goto, A., Goto, M., Inoue, M., Heianza, Y., Arase, Y., Sone, H., Nakagami, T., Song, X., Qiao, Q., Tuomilehto, J., Tsugane, S., Noda, M., & Inoue, M. (2015). Impact of population aging on trends in diabetes prevalence: A meta-regression analysis of 160,000 Japanese adults. Journal of Diabetes Investigation, 6(5), 533–542. https://doi.org/10.1111/jdi.12333

Chicken and vegetable salad wraps. (2016, March 15). Eat Smarter USA. https://eatsmarter.com/recipes/chicken-and-vegetable-salad-wraps

Chimenti, O. (2023, August 29). Sugar-free pumpkin chia pudding – I hacked diabetes. I Hacked Diabetes. https://ihackeddiabetes.com/pumpkin-chia-pudding/

Cinnamon honey cottage cheese. (2024). Eat This Much. https://www.eatthismuch.com/calories/cinnamon-honey-cottage-cheese-332567

Dahl, W. J., & Stewart, M. L. (2015). Position of the Academy of Nutrition and Dietetics: Health implications of dietary fiber. Journal of the Academy of Nutrition and Dietetics, 115(11), 1861–1870. https://doi.org/10.1016/j.jand.2015.09.003

DeAngelis, D. (2023, March 10). 17 easy high-protein breakfasts that aren't eggs. EatingWell. https://www.eatingwell.com/gallery/8034103/easy-high-protein-breakfasts-without-eggs/

Diabetes Care. (2023, September 10). 10 diabetes snacks. Diabetes Care Community. https://www.diabetescarecommunity.ca/diet-and-fitness-articles/10-diabetes-snacks/#:~:text=Enjoy%20hummus%20with%20your%20favourite%20raw%20vegetable%20sticks%3B

Diabetes Support. (2014). Greek salad with tofu recipe. https://www.diabetes-support.com/greek-salad-tofu-diabetic-recipe/

Diabetes UK. (n.d.). Healthy hummus. https://www.diabetes.org.uk/guide-to-diabetes/recipes/healthy-hummus

Diabetic tofu and vegetable stir-fry recipe. (n.d.). Diabetes Self-Management. https://www.diabetesselfmanagement.com/recipes/main-dishes/tofu-and-vegetable-stir-fry/

Dunnirvine, S. (2021, January 24). Salmon and broccoli stir fry. Garden in the Kitchen. https://garden-inthekitchen.com/salmon-and-broccoli-stir-fry/

Eat Live Run. (2011, August 2). Greek yogurt cheesecake. Tastykitchen.com. https://tastykitchen.com/recipes/desserts/greek-yogurt-cheesecake/

Food Network Kitchen. (2017, March 31). Grilled pork tenderloin and sweet potatoes. Food Network. https://www.foodnetwork.com/recipes/food-network-kitchen/grilled-pork-tenderloin-and-sweet-potatoes-3677245

Freer, C. (2017, March 14). Sticky roasted peaches with ricotta cream. Healthy Food Guide. https://www.healthyfood.com/healthy-recipes/sticky-roasted-peaches-with-ricotta-cream/

Goggins, L. (2022). Our 19 best lentil soup recipes to keep you warm & cozy. EatingWell. https://www.eatingwell.com/gallery/7944878/best-lentil-soup-recipes/

Grilled steaks and Brussels sprouts | certified Angus beef. (2024). Certified Angus Beef. https://www.certifiedangusbeef.com/en/cooking/recipes/Grilled-Steaks-and-Brussels-Sprouts

Homolka, G., & Jones, H. K. (2014). The skinnytaste cookbook. Clarkson Potter.

https://www.allrecipes.com/recipe/230690/avocado-and-black-bean-dip/. (2024). Avocado and black bean dip. Allrecipes. https://www.allrecipes.com/recipe/230690/avocado-and-black-bean-dip/

International Diabetes Federation. (2021). IDF Diabetes Atlas 2021 10th Edition. IDF Diabetes Atlas. https://diabetesatlas.org/atlas/tenth-edition/

Julia. (2020, January 23). Savory breakfast bowl recipe. Happy Foods Tube. https://www.happyfood-stube.com/savory-breakfast-bowl/

Katerina. (2017, May 15). Frozen yogurt bark with berries. Diethood. https://diethood.com/frozen-yogurt-bark/

Katrin Nürnberger. (2018, October 12). Chocolate avocado mousse (keto). Sugar-Free Londoner. https://sugarfreelondoner.com/chocolate-avocado-mousse/

Kelly. (2018, April 12). Baked egg cups - 8 ways. Life Made Sweeter. https://lifemadesweeter.com/baked-egg-cups/

Kim. (2020, August 18). Easy sugar-free lemon bars. My Sugar-Free Kitchen. https://www.mysugar-freekitchen.com/sugar-free-lemon-bars/

King, K. (2024, August 29). Chickpea and black bean snack mix. Dizzy Busy and Hungry! https://dizzy-busyandhungry.com/chickpea-black-bean-snack-mix/

Laseter, E. (2024, May 21). The last avocado toast recipe you'll ever need. EatingWell. https://www.eatingwell.com/recipe/8029771/avocado-toast-recipe/

Linnie. (2020, October 28). Sweet potato fries oven-baked recipe (perfectly cooked fries). Plant-Based Easy Recipes by Veggie Balance. https://www.veggiebalance.com/sweet-potato-fries-oven-baked/

Mäkinen, K. K. (2016). Gastrointestinal disturbances associated with the consumption of sugar alcohols with special consideration of xylitol: Scientific review and instructions for dentists and other health-care professionals. International Journal of Dentistry, 2016, 1–16. https://doi.org/10.1155/2016/5967907

Malcoun, C. (2023). Spinach & feta frittata. EatingWell. https://www.eatingwell.com/recipe/8050155/spinach-feta-frittata/

Mayo Clinic Staff. (2023). Diabetes diet: Create your healthy-eating plan. Mayo Clinic. https://www.mayoclinic.org/diseases-conditions/diabetes/in-depth/diabetes-diet/art-20044295

Morrison, G. (2021, March 5). Stuffed portobello mushrooms with spinach and feta. https://www.she-keepsalovelyhome.com/stuffed-portobello-mushrooms/

National Institute of Diabetes and Digestive and Kidney Diseases. (2018, May). Insulin resistance & prediabetes. NIH NIDDK. https://www.niddk.nih.gov/health-information/diabetes/overview/what-is-diabetes/prediabetes-insulin-resistance

Noronha, J. C., Braunstein, C. R., Glenn, A. J., Khan, T. A., Viguiliouk, E., Noseworthy, R., Sonia Blanco Mejía, Cyril W.C. Kendall, Thomas, Leiter, L. A., & Sievenpiper, J. L. (2018). The effect of small doses of fructose and allulose on postprandial glucose metabolism in type 2 diabetes: A double☒blind, randomized, controlled, acute feeding, equivalence trial. Diabetes, Obesity and Metabolism, 20(10), 2361–2370. https://doi.org/10.1111/dom.13374

Nuria. (2020, May 7). Almond flax seed muffins (gluten-free, low carb). Peonies and a Latte. https://www.peoniesandalatte.com/2020/05/almond-flax-seed-muffins-gluten-free.html

Nürnberger, K. (2023, September 21). Coconut flour blueberry muffins. Sugar-Free Londoner. https://sugarfreelondoner.com/coconut-blueberry-muffins/

O'Brien, D. (2024, January 30). The only chia seed pudding recipe you'll ever need. EatingWell. https://www.eatingwell.com/chia-seed-pudding-8430793

Oerum, C. (2016, August 27). Sugar-free cottage cheese parfait with berries. Diabetes Strong. https://diabetesstrong.com/sugar-free-cottage-cheese-parfait-berries/

Oerum, C. (2019a, May 8). Sugar-Free chocolate chip cookies (low-carb). Diabetes Strong. https://diabetesstrong.com/sugar-free-chocolate-chip-cookies-low-carb/

Oerum, C. (2019b, August 16). Low-carb eggplant parmesan. Diabetes Strong. https://diabetesstrong.com/low-carb-eggplant-parmesan/

Parker, J. (2024, March 9). Diabetes quinoa recipes. Diabetes Type One. https://diabetestypeone.com/diabetes-quinoa-recipes/

Petersen, M. C., & Shulman, G. I. (2018). Mechanisms of insulin action and insulin resistance. Physiological Reviews, 98(4), 2133–2223. https://doi.org/10.1152/physrev.00063.2017

Riolo, A. (2019). Mini vegetable frittata. American Diabetes Association's Diabetesfoodhub.org. https://diabetesfoodhub.org/recipes/mini-vegetable-frittata

Roberts, A. (2019, August 22). Low-carb raspberry muffins. Spinach Tiger. https://spinachtiger.com/keto-raspberry-muffins-recipe-almond-flour/

Rondinelli Hamilton, L. (2017). Zucchini noodles with turkey meatballs | american diabetes association. Diabetesfoodhub.org. https://diabetesfoodhub.org/recipes/zucchini-noodles-turkey-meatballs

Rorke, M. (2024, September 3). Easy u0026amp; Healthy Chicken Curry - Slow Cooker Recipe. Whole Hearty Kitchen. https://www.wholeheartykitchen.co.uk/healthy-chicken-curry-slow-cooker-recipe/

Rutledge, C. (2014). Gluten-free almond flour crackers. King Arthur Baking. https://www.kingarthur-baking.com/recipes/gluten-free-almond-flour-crackers-recipe

Sherrell, Z. (2023, May 26). 7 best sweeteners and sugar substitutes for people with diabetes. Medical News Today. https://www.medicalnewstoday.com/articles/323469

Skyler, J. S., Bakris, G. L., Bonifacio, E., Darsow, T., Eckel, R. H., Groop, L., Groop, P.-H., Handelsman, Y., Insel, R. A., Mathieu, C., McElvaine, A. T., Palmer, J. P., Pugliese, A., Schatz, D. A., Sosenko, J. M., Wilding, J. P. H., & Ratner, R. E. (2017). Differentiation of diabetes by pathophysiology, natural history, and prognosis. Diabetes, 66(2), 241–255. https://doi.org/10.2337/db16-0806

The Healthline Editorial Team. (2024, April 25). The best sugar substitutes for people with diabetes. Healthline. https://www.healthline.com/health/type-2-diabetes/diabetes-stevia

Turkey lettuce wraps for diabetics. (n.d.). Diabetes Self-Management. https://www.diabetesselfmanagement.com/recipes/main-dishes/turkey-lettuce-wraps/

Vegetable and cheese omelet recipe | how to make an omelet. (2013, May 14). Cooking Nook. https://www.cookingnook.com/recipe/omelet-recipe/

Verdi, C. L., & Dunbar, S. A. (2019). Diabetes superfoods cookbook and meal planner: Power-packed recipes and meal plans designed to help you lose weight and manage your blood glucose. American Diabetes Association.

Vespa, J. (2023, August 11). Mediterranean baked cod. Dishing out Health. https://dishingouthealth. com/mediterranean-baked-cod/

Volz, M. (2020, October 11). Actually, the best vegetarian chili recipe ever. Ambitious Kitchen. https:// www.ambitiouskitchen.com/best-vegetarian-chili-recipe/

Witkowski, M., Nemet, I., Alamri, H., Wilcox, J., Gupta, N., Nimer, N., Haghikia, A., Li, X. S., Wu, Y., Saha, P. P., Demuth, I., König, M., Steinhagen-Thiessen, E., Cajka, T., Fiehn, O., Landmesser, U., Tang, W. H. W., & Hazen, S. L. (2023). The artificial sweetener erythritol and cardiovascular event risk. Nature Medicine, 29, 1–9. https://doi.org/10.1038/s41591-023-02223-9

World Health Organization. (2016). Global report on diabetes. Geneva: WHO. https://apps.who.int/iris/ handle/10665/204871

Glycemic index chart supplied by The Diabetes Association of Canada

Made in the USA
Las Vegas, NV
09 December 2024